Trotsky's Notebooks, 1933–1935

Trotsky's Notebooks, 1933–1935

Writings on Lenin, Dialectics, and Evolutionism

Translated, Annotated,
and with Introductory Essays
by PHILIP POMPER

Russian Text Annotated
by YURI FELSHTINSKY

New York   Columbia University Press   1986

Trotskys Notobooks, 1933-1935:
Writings of Lenin, Dialectics and Evolutionism

All Rights Reserved. Copyright © 1998 Philip Pomper

No part of this book may be reproduced or transmitted in any form or by any means, graphic, electronic, or mechanical, including photocopying, recording, taping, or by any information storage or retrieval system, without the permission in writing from the publisher.

This edition republished by arrangement with toExcel Press an imprint of iUniverse.com, Inc.

For information address:
iUniverse.com, Inc.
620 North 48th Street
Suite 201
Lincoln, NE 68504-3467
www.iuniverse.com

ISBN: 1-58348-115-x

Library of Congress Catalog Card Number: 98-89839

Printed in the United States of America

Contents

Acknowledgments	vii
Introduction	1
1. Notes on Lenin and Revolutionary Politics	17
2. Notes on Dialectics and Evolutionism	37
3. The Notebooks in Translation	75
Notebook on Hegel	75
The Second Notebook	79
Additional Notes on Dialectics and Darwinism: Discussion and Translation	108
4. Russian Text of the Notebook on Hegel	117
5. Russian Text of the Second Notebook	121
6. Russian Text of the Additional Notes	150
Notes	157
Annotations to the English Translations	165
Index	171

Acknowledgments

Trotsky's notebooks, the additional notes, and the photographs are published by permission of the Houghton Library, Harvard University.

The research and writing for this project were undertaken and completed in the academic year 1984–85 during a sabbatical and leave from Wesleyan University. I am particularly indebted to my colleagues in the Department of History for supporting me with a grant from the Meigs Fund. The Russian Research Center of Harvard University facilitated my work by making me a Visiting Scholar, giving me access to the resources of the center and the Harvard library system. The staff of the Houghton Library at Harvard, where the bulk of Trotsky's papers are deposited, graciously and efficiently expedited my research; I thank the library for granting me permission to publish the notebooks. I would also like to thank Saundra Taylor of the Lilly Library of Indiana University for her help with the Trotsky-Eastman manuscripts there.

I presented some of the ideas and material contained in this book to the Historians' Seminar at the Russian Research Center and the University Seminar on Slavic History and Culture at Columbia University. Among those who encouraged me, commented on the material during its composition, or raised stimulating questions I would like particularly to thank Loren Graham and Doug Wiener, who advised me about the material on evolutionism, Paul Avrich, Abe Ascher, Dan Mulholland, Oliver W. Holmes, and Charles Lemert. My thanks also go to Jean van Heijenoort for our long talk about Trotsky and for his interest in the project. It was my good fortune to meet Yuri Felshtinsky in the Houghton Library. I am grateful to him for spending quite a few hours with me deciphering Trotsky's handwriting, going over the translation, and preparing the Russian text.

I am indebted to Fran Warren and my wife Alice for their work on the manuscript. My special thanks go to Kate Wittenberg and Anne McCoy at Columbia University Press, who provided the kind of editorial help without which such projects would never be realized in their best form.

Philip Pomper
Middletown, Connecticut

Trotsky's Notebooks, 1933–1935

Introduction

This project emerged unexpectedly, as is often the case when one is able to work freely and without interruption with archival materials. During research for a future work on the relations among Lenin, Trotsky, and Stalin in the period after the revolution of 1917, I conducted a systematic survey of the materials Trotsky had been collecting for a biography of Lenin. They are part of the vast collection of Trotsky documents that Harvard University acquired during the 1940s, all of which are deposited in the manuscript collection of Houghton Library. The notebooks on Lenin and dialectics had not been closed to researchers until 1980, as had been the case with a designated section of Trotsky's archives. They are contained in white folders and classified bMSRuss13 T3825 and T3826.

The first notebook, T3825, is 22 × 17 cm, has a light-blue cardboard cover, and contains forty-six stapled leaves. They are lined, and there is a margin 3 cm wide on the left, but Trotsky disregarded the margin and used the space to its left. The first notebook contains material on Hegel, mainly excerpts from the first part of Hegel's *Wissenschaft der Logik* with Trotsky's comments. "Hegel" is written on the front cover (without quotation marks) with Cyrillic letters in blue pencil and underlined. The capital is approximately 2 cm high and the lowercase letters, approximately 1 cm. Only five pages are used: both sides of two leaves and one side of another. Except for one insertion in ink on the first page, and the material on the last page, the notebook on Hegel is written entirely in pencil. It ends abruptly, apparently in midsentence, because the last punctuation mark is a comma after the word "process."

The second notebook, T3826, is 21½ × 17 cm and contains forty-seven leaves (without a margin), which are sewn into glossy, tan cardboard covers. The Cyrillic capital "L" (3 cm high) is written in red pencil on the front cover over a logo with "GALLIA" underneath. It undoubtedly stands for "Lenin." There is an oval with "Librairies R. Lefevre" and an illegible word, probably the location of the bookstore, affixed by a rubber stamp in purple ink on the back cover, upper left. Eighty-one pages of the second notebook have been used, although sometimes they contain very little—two or three lines. The last five leaves and three other pages are completely blank. This notebook too is written largely in pencil. Trotsky used mainly graphite, but there are comments and markings in red and blue pencil as well—Trotsky's characteristic notations for calling attention to important sections of the text. An entry in ink on the forty-eighth page under the newspaper clipping of June 5 [1934] announces Enrico Fermi's creation of an artificial element, an insertion which supports Trotsky's dating of the second notebook. He wrote "1933–1934" (underlined, without quotation marks) at the top of the second leaf (the first page used) in the upper left-hand corner. The last seven pages of text, one of which is cut, are also in ink, and they also appear after a newspaper clipping, this one announcing the plans for the tricentenary celebration of Descartes' *Discourse on Method.* In addition, a typed passage containing material from a Russian journal is pasted into the second notebook on the sixty-third page.

The handwriting in the notebook varies from a loose scrawl written in pencil, to more careful and tighter letters written in ink. Trotsky's handwriting reflected the instrument used and, no doubt, his own intentions. He was quite conscious about handwriting, as will be clear from his comments about graphology and Lenin's handwriting in the second notebook. In any case, the handwriting matches numerous other samples in a large number of documents. This is not only my opinion, but that of Yuri Felshtinsky, who has also been working with Trotsky materials and has published a number of Trotsky's works in Russian for the first

Introduction 3

time. In addition, I have discussed the notebooks with Jean van Heijenoort, Trotsky's secretary and bodyguard during the 1930s, who wrote the foreword to the Trotsky notebooks published by Harvard University Press in 1976 under the title *Trotsky's Diary in Exile, 1935*.

After a run through of the notebooks, I found myself stumped over a number of words. Mr. Felshtinsky, who is a native speaker of Russian, was able to decipher most of the words that I could not, and I decided to ask him to collaborate on the preparation of a Russian text. We worked together over the most difficult words. In the end, we were able to agree about all but a few words, which neither of us could read. Russian is a highly declined language, and Trotsky often failed to complete words, leaving it to the unlucky reader to figure things out from the context. Unfortunately, contexts are sometimes too incomplete themselves to yield answers, but in most cases we felt confident that we had supplied correct endings. They are contained in brackets in the Russian text.

In addition, Trotsky left out letters in words and made grammatical errors, which no doubt issued from changes of mind in midsentence. He simply did not go back over the sentence in order to achieve total accuracy, as he did in the drafts of works intended for publication. Here again, Mr. Felshtinsky has supplied corrections in brackets and annotations to indicate the errors. After thorough discussion of every doubtful case, we agreed that this is as close to an accurate Russian text as we could jointly achieve. Readers who wish to see what Trotsky crossed out (and was still legible) may consult the Russian text. I simply omitted words or phrases crossed out by Trotsky when they were obviously false starts and superfluous. When he crossed out material that I thought interesting and substantive I placed it in parentheses enclosed by brackets at its proper place in the text. The annotations to the Russian text are in the form of Mr. Felshtinsky's linguistic and textual clarifications in footnotes. My annotations to the English text are in the form of notes gathered at the end of the book.

In my English translation I have occasionally made insertions, also in brackets, when I have felt that a slight addition might make the text clearer. I have also inserted punctuation where it was needed, but did not resort to brackets. Everything else is wholly Trotsky's. Mr. Felshtinsky checked my translation, and we believe that we have provided English-language readers with a fair rendering of Trotsky's ideas. Of course, the usual apologies for trying to translate an outstanding prose style into another language are in order here. But it should be emphasized that these are notes, that Trotsky ordinarily worked more at perfecting his prose, and that in view of the centrality of philosophical issues, accuracy of translation was the major concern. Even so, Trotsky's prose is quite fluent and shows his characteristic use of metaphor and analogy.

In my opinion, the final pages of the second notebook contain the most developed and original ideas, although they are quite tentative and seem too slight to carry the burden of the weighty philosophical problems undertaken by Trotsky. Yet it is their very tentativeness that gives them value, in this case, because they do not suffer from the constraints of political discourse. Trotsky's rhetorical brilliance and polemical skill served him well in revolutionary politics, but they tended to diminish his philosophical statements, to lead to oversimplifications. Like Lenin's *Philosophical Notebooks,* Trotsky's show freshness of thought and express the delight of intellectual discovery; and like Lenin's, Trotsky's notebooks on philosophical problems do him greater credit as a thinker than his published works on dialectics.

The "Additional Notes" are contained among other materials in the folder T3749—also part of the collection connected with Trotsky's biography of Lenin. They are clearly related to the material in the notebooks, although they are written or typed on seventeen separate sheets of typing paper of standard size. Some of the sheets have been cut into slips that are half-size or smaller. The notes are written mainly in ink, in clearer handwriting than that of the notebooks, and there are two typed pages. Mr. Felshtinsky and I followed the same procedures with the scattered notes as we did with the two notebooks. However, the headings on most of the notes were repetitious. They have been omitted and the notes grouped under the correct headings.

Introduction

My essays on the notebooks and the additional notes are designed to connect them with earlier and later works and to explicate them, not only by examining the ideas, but by seeking in Trotsky's career a more complex understanding of their meaning. Thus, the exposition is not simply an exercise in the history of ideas, but an effort to understand their personal as well as historical background. Trotsky's autobiography proved to be invaluable for this part of the project, and it was my good fortune to be able to check the published text against an unpublished draft with Trotsky's handwritten corrections. Sometimes material that has been crossed out can be illuminating. Trotsky's notes for his biography of Stalin, only selected parts of which were added to the finished parts of the manuscript by the translator and editor, Charles Malamuth, also proved to be valuable. In addition, I have used the Trotsky-Eastman correspondence contained in the Lilly Library of Indiana University. Mainly letters for the period 1929–33, they supplement correspondence in the Trotsky Archives. The Trotsky-Eastman correspondence sheds light on Trotsky's planned biography of Lenin and on Trotsky's motives for his investigation of dialectics. I have not attempted a full analysis of Trotsky's personality, but have presented suggestive material and offered hypotheses about the notes toward the unfinished biography of Lenin and about Trotsky's style as a dialectician. It is my hope that readers who already know Trotsky well will feel that they know him better after reading what follows. For readers with less background, I provide the following sketch as a framework for the discussion of the notebooks and for the notebooks themselves.

Trotsky's Career: A Thumbnail Sketch

Leon Trotsky is the revolutionary pseudonym taken by Lev Bronstein. "Leon" could as easily be rendered "Lev," but it has become customary to use the former, and the custom will be followed here. Trotsky was born of Jewish parents in the Ukraine in 1879. Unlike most Jewish youths, Trotsky grew up on a farm. His ambitious father, a *kulak,* or rich farmer by the standards of the peasants of the Russian empire, wanted the boy to expand and modernize the family enterprise and sent him away to school at the age of nine. Trotsky showed extraordinary ability as a student, but his early ambition to become a mathematician gave way to a quest for social justice. At the age of sixteen, after six years of schooling in the Black Sea port of Odessa, the young Trotsky traveled in 1896 to the city of Nikolaev to continue his secondary education. After completing his studies in 1897, he entered the University of Odessa, but, like many other young intellectuals, found himself drawn to the revolutionary movement. He joined one of the many circles of young people seeking to overturn the Tsarist regime and establish a new social order, one satisfying the new "scientific" theories of history and society current among the European intelligentsia. In March 1897 he began his revolutionary career in Nikolaev.

An indigenous school of historical sociology had developed the idea of a scientific ethic during the 1860s and 1870s. The notion that socialism satisfied both science and ethics had become an article of faith among Russian radical thinkers. Furthermore, Russian thinkers believed that relative economic backwardness might be a blessing in disguise, for it had permitted Russia to preserve a form of collectivism practiced by the peasants in their repartitional communes. It remained to liberate the peasants from Tsarist tyranny and exploitation by landlords, and to prevent modern capitalism from destroying the communes. The views of the populist intelligentsia still prevailed during Trotsky's early adolescence. However, the Russian intelligentsia had long debated different socialist theories. By the mid-1890s, Russian Marxists had achieved some success in challenging the belief that the peasant repartitional commune might serve as the basis for a progressive socialist order. Trotsky began his adolescent career as a populist—a proponent of agrarian socialism issuing from the socialist inclinations of the peasants—but became a Marxist in 1897. He thenceforth remained committed to the idea that a class of exploited factory workers, landless proletarians, would overturn

Introduction 7

unjust social orders and create a new socialist society. The Marxian inspiration remained strong in him until his death in 1940.

Trotsky was first arrested in January 1898 for illegal pamphleteering and propaganda connected with his activities as the leading figure in the South Russian Workers' Union. After more than a year and a half in prison in Odessa, and then six months in Moscow, where he married Alexandra Sokolovskaia, he was sentenced to a four-year term of exile in Siberia. By 1902 Sokolovskaia had given birth to two daughters, but seemed resigned to the idea that Trotsky should escape and pursue his career and that she should carry on alone. He fled Siberia in September 1902. Even during Siberian exile, he had developed his skills as a writer and produced a series of reviews for an Irkutsk journal. When he reached London in October 1902, he was not without reputation. However, he was still a novice compared to the illustrious émigrés who had founded the journal *Iskra* (Spark) and created the theoretical bases for Russian Marxism: Plekhanov, Zasulich, Aksel'rod, Martov, Potresov, and—Lenin. He quickly became a collaborator on the journal.

Like many others in the Russian Social Democratic Workers' Party, Trotsky was shocked by the disagreement over the editorial board of *Iskra* and the organization of the socialist workers' party that split the Russian Marxists into Bolsheviks and Mensheviks in 1903. Lenin's "hard"—that is, centralist and conspiratorial—ideas of organization repelled those who became Mensheviks. His position smacked of Jacobin dictatorship and contradicted the idea that a spontaneous workers' movement would achieve revolutionary consciousness and provide its own leadership. Trotsky was repelled by Lenin's tactics and joined the attack. Despite the fact that Lenin called his faction "Bolshevik," majoritarian, the Menshevik, presumably the minority faction, in fact was the dominant one after 1903, and Martov became its leading theoretician. Trotsky attacked Lenin vehemently in a brochure written in 1904 and remained alienated from the Bolshevik faction throughout his years in exile. However, he found it impossible (largely thanks to Plekhanov's hostility) to establish a continuous relationship with the Mensheviks either, and after a brief collaboration on Martov's *Iskra,* began to pursue an independent line.

During 1904 he traveled to Munich and placed himself under the tutelage of Alexander Helphand, a cosmopolitan socialist who went under the revolutionary pseudonym "Parvus," and whose intellectual and political insight inspired Trotsky at a transitional moment of his career. In 1905 Trotsky returned along with other émigrés to join the impressive movement that peaked in the autumn of that year and subsided only after the Tsar in October was forced to grant a parliamentary system, which proved to be fragile. During the course of the revolution of 1905, spontaneous sociopolitical forms arose in all social strata, but the soviets, representative councils elected mainly by factory workers, proved to be the most historically significant one. Members of revolutionary parties found willing listeners and acquired instantaneous celebrity as orators and leaders in the gatherings of the St. Petersburg Soviet. Trotsky already exhibited the charismatic qualities that made him one of the central figures in 1917, and was the leader of the soviet during its brief existence in the autumn of 1905 before the government of Nicholas II recovered and arrested the leaders.

After imprisonment in December 1905, trial in the autumn of 1906, and a brief period of Siberian exile in February 1907, Trotsky once again escaped and fled abroad. The post-1905 period of exile was long and painful for the revolutionaries who had experienced 1905, had seen a promising revolutionary situation repressed, and now anxiously watched the recovery of the regime under the leadership of Prime Minister Peter Stolypin. The period 1907–14 is generally characterized as a period of defeat and stagnation for Russian revolutionaries, although the labor movement began to revive in 1912. Trotsky refused to tie himself to either Mensheviks or Bolsheviks throughout this period and showed a spirit of independence that proved to be simultaneously a strength and a weakness. On the one hand, it apparently permitted him to develop his own vision, not, to be sure, in isolation, but free from the entanglements of factionalism. On the other, his lack of firm ties to any party or faction had serious political consequences

Introduction

in the long run, and he never acquired the thick skin necessary for political infighting.

During 1904–6, inspired by Parvus and the Russian revolution of 1905, he had formulated the theory of permanent revolution, a theory that signified a kind of permanent revolutionary optimism. Trotsky justified revolution in relatively backward nations like Russia by seeing it as part of a structure of relationships within world capitalism. The Russian bourgeoisie's weakness would permit the still young proletariat to overthrow it prematurely, so to speak. But the problem of foreshortening the bourgeois stage of history could still be solved. The Russian proletariat would give the signal to the proletariat of the advanced nations. They would lead the class struggle of the world proletariat. Lenin later arrived at a similar position through his analysis of imperialism. Russia, the weak link in the chain of capitalist imperialist powers, would snap in the process of revolution, and start the process of disintegration of the world capitalist order. The proletariat of advanced industrial nations would expropriate the expropriators and share the benefits of accumulated technology and wealth with the proletarians of relatively backward nations. This vision put both Trotsky and Lenin on the left of the European socialist movement in general, and of the Russian Social Democratic Workers' Party in particular, especially after the outbreak of the First World War. It gave them a basis for collaboration in 1917. However, they remained estranged until 1917.

After his second escape from Siberian exile in 1907, Trotsky earned his living mainly as a journalist for both socialist and nonsocialist periodicals, and for a time edited his own journal, *Pravda* (1908–12), before the Bolsheviks printed their journal of the same title—a provocation which only further alienated him from them. He lived in Vienna, immersed himself in its lively political and cultural life, and became acquainted with the psychoanalytic movement. He also traveled in connection with socialist politics and was thoroughly cosmopolitan in his inclinations. Trotsky now had two sons by his second wife, Natalia Sedova, with whom he had established a relationship during a visit to Paris in 1902. They remained together for the remainder of Trotsky's life. The story of Trotsky's two families cannot be told here, but it is difficult to imagine Trotsky enduring his last exile without Natalia Sedova's support. Their mutual devotion and love sustained them through several family tragedies.

The outbreak of World War I began three years of global wandering for Trotsky. Expelled from Austria in August 1914, he traveled to Switzerland where he remained until November of that year, then to France for a sojourn of two years. While in Paris Trotsky collaborated uneasily with Martov on the journal *Nashe slovo* (Our Word), but as coeditor he was able to pursue his own line. In September 1915 in Zimmerwald, Switzerland, thirty-eight socialist internationalists convened to develop a policy independent of that of the Second International; Trotsky drafted the group's manifesto. Throughout this period, and during the Zimmerwald Conference as well, Trotsky and Lenin remained opponents, despite the narrowing of the difference between their positions. After expulsion from France in October 1916, Trotsky ended his westward European trek in Spain, and in December disembarked from Cadiz for the United States. He resided in New York City and worked as a journalist for *Novyi mir* (New World), an émigré journal, until mid-March 1917, when he began his trip back to Russia. On the return voyage he was briefly interned in Canada, and reached revolutionary Petrograd only in May 1917, one month after Lenin's arrival.

Unable to bear the strains of World War I, the Tsarist regime had finally disintegrated in March 1917. As in 1905, the revolutionary émigrés found themselves drawn back to Russia. But this time the Romanov dynasty fell and a provisional government was installed. Lenin and Trotsky finally found a basis for collaboration. Trotsky's leadership of the Petrograd Soviet and the Military Revolutionary Committee played a central role in the Bolshevik seizure of power in October 1917. After enrollment as a Bolshevik in August 1917, he became Lenin's partner in revolutionary leadership—a closer partner than members of long standing in the Bolshevik Central Committee. He was laden with heavy responsibilities from the very beginning: As the first Com-

Introduction

missar of Foreign Affairs of the new Soviet government in 1917 he had to conduct the negotiations for a peace treaty with the Germans and Austrians at Brest-Litovsk; shortly after that painful assignment, he became the Commissar of War, responsible for the organization of the Red Army and much of the strategy of the Civil War. Trotsky achieved international fame in these roles. The survival of the Soviet regime guaranteed Trotsky a place in history.

However, in the prosecution of his governmental duties, Trotsky once again found himself fighting with the Bolshevik leadership. Lenin had learned how to use Trotsky's administrative talent, but he could not make Trotsky acceptable to all the old Bolsheviks. The enmity between Trotsky and Stalin grew during ugly confrontations over the conduct of military affairs in the Civil War. Stalin, an old Bolshevik, found Trotsky insufferably arrogant; Trotsky found Stalin crude and talentless. Their mutual lack of respect and Stalin's envy had major political consequences. Before his illness, Lenin could control the struggles within the Bolshevik Central Committee and eventually get his way. But the Party was bitterly divided over major policy issues. Trotsky had often taken controversial positions, sometimes backed by Lenin, sometimes opposed by him: in the Civil War he had used former Tsarist officers; his initial position on peace had given the Germans the opportunity to seize more Russian territory in 1918; he had used parts of the army as labor units, in an effort to "militarize" labor at the end of the Civil War; he had prematurely proposed a partial return to free trade, and when later the New Economic Policy had been adopted, he had quickly criticized it; he had proposed a form of governmental administration of the trade unions that would have immediately deprived them of any autonomy. Trotsky's outspoken promotion of unpopular policies and his poor timing as a politician might have been forgivable if he had had longer standing in the Party. However, by 1921, a major turning point in Soviet history, he had made many enemies.

At the end of the Civil War, Lenin's government and party faced a ruined economy and rebellion by the peasantry. A mutiny of the units stationed at the Kronstadt naval fortress in the Gulf of Finland forced Lenin to decide quickly to reverse the policy of War Communism of the period 1918–21 and to restore, at least partially, a market economy. However, despite the loosening of economic controls, Lenin created tighter political controls, destroying the remaining opposition outside the Party and establishing a ban on factions within it. The regime acted aggressively against any perceived political threat. Trotsky played a central role in the suppression of the mutiny at Kronstadt in March 1921. During the entire period of the Civil War he had acquired a reputation for ruthlessness that seemed to overshadow his reputation as charismatic leader, organizer, and administrator in the Party itself. Lenin had sometimes supported and sometimes opposed him. More generally, Lenin had used him, as he had used many others, as troubleshooters, in a series of situations which demanded people who could make ruthless decisions. Stalin too had played such roles, but had also taken over much of the day-to-day organizational work of the Party apparatus after 1922, as its general secretary. Stalin converted that and his other bureaucratic positions into key political ones by creating a circular flow of power—using appointments to secure support for his policies at Party congresses and in the Central Committee of the Party. But Stalin's own ruthlessness as Commissar of Nationalities infuriated Lenin in 1922, at a time when Lenin was already largely incapacitated from a stroke. Both Trotsky and Lenin saw Stalin in a new light. Trotsky, who had become a proponent of centralism, now saw its dangers.

Between 1922 and Lenin's death in 1924, Trotsky failed to arrest the growth of Stalin's power, even though the ailing Lenin joined the attack against Stalin. Stalin knew how to maneuver within the Party and how to form alliances with others who resented Trotsky, most notably, G. Zinoviev and L. Kamenev, the two members of the Politburo, who, along with Trotsky, were seen as Lenin's likely successors. Trotsky by 1923 had become an outsider—an oppositionist—and increasingly open to charges of factionalism. He opposed the New Economic Policy and the growing power of the Party apparatus, although his own plan for the economy seemed to suggest the need for coercion. Throughout the

Introduction 13

struggle, Trotsky failed to use whatever political advantage his alliance with Lenin against Stalin might have given him. He fell ill in 1923 and failed to attend Lenin's funeral in January 1924, a ceremonial blunder with political consequences. Furthermore, he was unable to use Lenin's "Testament" effectively. The multiple reasons for Trotsky's fall from power cannot be analyzed here, nor is it possible to discuss the question, did he really stand a chance to replace Lenin as the leader of the Party? One thing is certain: Stalin had become the master of the Party apparatus and disposed of both Trotsky and his own former allies against Trotsky when he no longer needed them.

Between 1925 and 1927, Trotsky acquired a large number of powerful allies, including Zinoviev and Kamenev, but they also failed to understand how far the apparatus had extended its control. Stalin was able to pursue his policies with impunity, despite major foreign policy defeats and warnings from the left opposition about the failure of NEP. He stripped his opponents of their own power bases. Trotsky had lost his positions as Commissar of War and President of the Revolutionary Military Council by January 1925. However, he still held administrative posts and remained in the Party's top policy organ, the Politburo, during 1925–27. The new alliance, called the "Joint Opposition," openly challenged the Party in the summer of 1926, but Stalin firmly controlled the Politburo and Central Committee. The opposition, led by Trotsky, suffered a continuous series of defeats, ending with Trotsky's expulsion from the Central Committee in October 1927. Their appeal to the rank and file in the streets of Leningrad during the celebration of the tenth anniversary of the October Revolution on November 7, 1927, ended in disaster, and led finally to Trotsky's expulsion from the Party on November 14.

Trotsky once again had become estranged from the Party. He was deported with his family to Alma Ata in central Asia in January 1928, and after a year there, in February 1929 was exiled to Turkey. He took up residence on the island of Prinkipo, in the sea of Marmora near Constantinople. Here he wrote some of his most brilliant books: his autobiography, *My Life,* and *The History of the Russian Revolution.* Here and later in France, Norway, and

Mexico he tried to revive the "degenerated" revolution by establishing his own journal, *The Bulletin of the Opposition,* and his own movement, the Fourth International. The rise of Fascism and Hitler's consolidation of power in 1933 convinced him to take a new course, previously unintended, as the revolutionary leader of a new party. Trotsky's new role coincided roughly with his move from Prinkipo to France. In July 1933 he began his period of exile in France. During this period, from July 1933 to May 1935, Trotsky made the entries in the two notebooks published here and also kept his diary for 1935 in notebooks of similar format. Trotsky left France for Norway in June 1935, and after another sojourn of a year and a half, was forced to leave for Mexico, his last place of exile, where he lived between January 1937 and his murder in August 1940.

Trotsky's life was punctuated by a series of ideological and political conversions, deconversions, and reversals of fortune. In *My Life,* written in 1928–29, there is a chapter entitled "The Break." It describes his year in Nikolaev, the period 1896–97, when he jumped from one book to another, one system of thought to another, before settling on Marxism. In his own retrospective assessment, he had been extremely ambivalent about submitting to a "system." He once told Max Eastman, who started a biography of him, that he had worried about his mental health because as a youth he couldn't make up his mind. Perhaps Trotsky had in mind the period in Nikolaev. Whatever the case, once he *did* make up his mind, once he had chosen revolution over pure mathematics as his vocation, and Marxism over Populism as his system, Trotsky remained firmly committed until the end of his life. This suggests not so much indecisiveness as a very limited tolerance for uncertainty—and a need for system exceeding the ordinary adolescent search for meaning. Among revolutionary careers, Trotsky's is a model of stable commitment. The vicissitudes of his political biography are what one might expect of the revolutionary vocation and the historical milieu. During the period 1929–40, his third and last period of foreign exile, he not only struggled to formulate a correct political position, but to create an image of the revolutionary past which would simultaneously satisfy his system and

Introduction

justify his earlier political decisions. In the end, Trotsky's achievements as a revolutionary leader, important though they undoubtedly were, may prove to be less impressive than his creation of an image of the Russian Revolution and its leaders which could both ease the pain of exile and promise ultimate victory.

1. Notes on Lenin and Revolutionary Politics

Trotsky's project for a biography of Lenin had a long prehistory. His correspondence with Max Eastman, his ambivalent disciple, translator, and literary agent during the 1930s, sheds considerable light on his initial plans. Trotsky by June 1929 had already agreed to write three books for the publisher of Eastman's book *Marx and Lenin: The Science of Revolution*. The first, on Lenin, was to have consisted of four parts: a biographical section; a section on his personality; one devoted to memoirs about him; and a collection of hundreds of letters by and to him during the period of the Russian Civil War and its aftermath. He hoped to finish the book, provisionally entitled *Lenin and the Epigones,* by the autumn of 1929.[1] In it, Trotsky also intended to answer some of Eastman's criticisms of Marxism in the book mentioned above. Trotsky eventually withdrew from his agreement with the publisher and a German publisher to whom he had offered *Lenin and the Epigones* as the first in a series of ten books.[2] Then in January 1931 he revealed his plan to write a book of political portraits entitled *They and We,* in which he would juxtapose a series of bourgeois or petit-bourgeois conservative politicians to proletarian revolutionaries. He had been provoked by Count Carlo Sforza's book *Makers of Modern Europe,* which contained an unflattering portrait of Lenin.[3] What Trotsky failed to mention in his letter of January 2 to Eastman was Sforza's chapter on the reasons for Trotsky's political failure and Stalin's victory, in which there are some devastatingly accurate observations about Trotsky's weaknesses.[4]

The depth of Trotsky's identification of himself with Lenin, his need to defend their mutual achievement, is suggested repeatedly in Trotsky's published writings. Two unpublished pieces of evidence are also germane here. When he first mentioned his project on Lenin to Eastman he wrote, "This book will represent, as it were, a continuation of the autobiography."[5] The second is an odd mistake appearing at the very beginning of Trotsky's second notebook, in which he describes a confrontation between Lenin and the Mensheviks in 1904. When describing Lenin's uncertainty he slips into the first person and describes his own self-doubt. In his own mind, he and Lenin were linked together.

Instead of devoting himself to a book on Lenin, however, Trotsky spent most of his literary efforts during his period of exile in Turkey on *The History of the Russian Revolution*. In it Lenin's role as leader overshadows his own. The other projects mentioned by Trotsky in his letters to Eastman were never realized for a number of reasons—not the least of them a fire in his villa on Prinkipo on March 1, 1931. It destroyed not only Trotsky's library but the materials he had been collecting for the proposed book of political portraits and others as well. The setback was only temporary, for Trotsky eventually replaced his losses, but a book on Lenin was out of the question for the time being. Trotsky returned to it after the trip to France in July 1933, and after his recovery from a fairly extended period of illness during the summer and fall of that year. The notebook with the "L." on the front cover and the date "1933–1934" is undoubtedly part of the Lenin project, but it is connected with a quarrel with Max Eastman over dialectics as well. Perhaps Trotsky had intended to use the notebook mainly for notes on Lenin's political career. If so, he changed course, because dialectics and evolutionism occupy the most prominent place in the notebook. The sketchy and epigrammatic character of the notes on Lenin encourage selective focus and interpretation, both of which will be evident in the treatment below.

The notes on Lenin reflect Trotsky's resumption of his ef-

Lenin and Revolutionary Politics

fort to form a coherent image of Lenin's personality and to connect that image with Lenin's political actions. Trotsky uses a dialectical method in the notebooks similar to the one he had planned to use in his book of political portraits, in that he juxtaposes Lenin to a series of opponents. The devastating thumbnail sketches of Plekhanov and Martov call to mind similarly brief but evocative studies of political figures in Trotsky's *History of the Russian Revolution*. However, Trotsky preferred the large canvas. This seems to be the import of the following remarks in a letter dated April 27, 1930, to Max Eastman: "I'm working on 'The History of 1917.' This is not simply a return to the past. on a large historical canvas you can represent in more concrete and convincing form a whole series of the most important strategic and tactical positions."[6] All his major writings subordinate biography to economic, social, and political history, as one might expect from one of the most talented historians ever to write history from the Marxian perspective. Even his lengthier biographical sketches are of modest dimensions. They have been collected into a single slim volume.[7] Nonetheless, Trotsky recognized the role of the individual in history and toward the end of the period when he was writing the notebooks took a seemingly unambiguous position about Lenin's crucial role in the October Revolution: It simply would not have occurred without Lenin. On March 25 he wrote in the diary that he kept during 1935:

> Had I not been present in 1917 in Petersburg, the October Revolution would still have taken place—*on the condition that Lenin was present and in command.* If neither Lenin nor I had been present in Petersburg, there would have been no October Revolution: the leadership of the Bolshevik Party would have prevented it from occurring—of this I have not the slightest doubt![8]

It is instructive to compare the above statement about Lenin's role in the October Revolution with an earlier statement, written roughly five years earlier, in *The History of the Russian Revolution*:

> How would the revolution have developed if Lenin had not reached Russia in April 1917? If our exposition demonstrates and proves anything at all, we hope it proves that Lenin was not a demiurge

of the revolutionary process, that he merely entered into a chain of objective historic forces. But he was a great link in that chain. The dictatorship of the proletariat was to be inferred from the whole situation, but it had to be established. It could not be established without a party. The party could fulfill its mission only after understanding it. For that Lenin was needed. . . . Is it possible, however, to say confidently that the party without him would have found its road? We would by no means make bold to say that. . . . The role of personality arises before us here on a truly gigantic scale. It is necessary only to understand that role correctly, taking personality as a link in the historic chain.[9]

Trotsky's own biographer, Isaac Deutscher, himself a Marxian dialectician, believed that Trotsky had been suffering from an "optical illusion" when he had written the two passages quoted above, and tried to save Trotsky from inadvertent betrayal of the Marxian perspective by quoting Trotsky's later work *The Revolution Betrayed*. There Trotsky emphasized the "correlation of social forces" and "obedience to objective law" and seemed to say that the quality of leadership was not the decisive factor.[10] In his posthumously published biography of Stalin, Trotsky provided still another variation on the theme of Lenin's role, in which he tried to arrive at a balanced formulation of the relationship of Lenin's genius to the character of the Party:

A revolutionist of Lenin's makeup and breadth could be the leader only of the most fearless party, capable of carrying its thoughts and actions to their logical conclusion. But genius in itself is the rarest of exceptions. A leader of genius orients himself faster, estimates the situation more thoroughly, sees further than others. It was unavoidable that a great gap should develop between the leader of genius and his closest collaborators. It may even be conceded that to a certain extent the very power of Lenin's vision acted as a brake on the development of self-reliance among his collaborators. Nevertheless, that does not mean that Lenin was "everything" and the Party without Lenin was nothing. Without the Party Lenin would have been as helpless as Darwin and Newton without collective scientific work. . . . The leader of genius is important because, in shortening the learning period by means of object lessons, he enables the party to influence the development of events at the proper moment. Had Lenin failed to come at the beginning of April, no doubt the Party would have groped its way eventually to the course propounded in his "Theses." But could anyone else have prepared the Party in time for the October denouement? The question cannot be answered categorically.[11]

In any case, when Trotsky wrote the diary entry about Lenin's role in the October Revolution, he reinforced the position that he had taken earlier in his history of the revolution and other works. We may surmise that Trotsky's conviction about Lenin's importance, if anything, had grown during 1933–35 when he was writing the notebooks, collecting materials for the biography, composing the first part of it, and keeping his diary.

Trotsky had scarcely seen the third and last volume of his history of the revolution in print when he returned to his project to rescue Lenin's historical image from the historiography of the "epigones" and the treatment of outsiders like Sforza. The unpublished notes for a foreword to his projected biography of Lenin, although sketchy, clarify both his motives and his method as a biographer. Trotsky characterized the historiography of the epigones in these terms:

> Lenin had no predecessors, or else they were pushed aside into the deepest shadows. In addition, Lenin's own intellectual life ceases to be a process of development. It has no stages, crises, sharp breaks, mistakes, and corrections. Lenin's life consists of automatic expositions and applications 'of Bolshevism's fundamental positions.'
>
> Epigonism signifies a suspension of intellectual growth. The historiography of epigonism extends this stagnation to the past as well. Once Leninism had appeared upon the earth it remained unchanging. . . .[12]

Trotsky loaded the word "epigone" with contempt. It signified for him the degeneration of the Russian Revolution, the transfer of power into the hands of inferior leadership. A relentless ambition to present the true picture of the Russian Revolution and to justify himself lay behind Trotsky's extraordinary literary productivity during the years of his exile on the Turkish island of Prinkipo between February 1929 and July 1933. Although the epigones had political power and control over Soviet historiography, Trotsky still had the power of his pen—a power to create a different image of history, of Lenin's historical role, and of Trotsky's connection to both. Trotsky had a profound faith that he, and perhaps only he, could present a true image of the Revolution and its leadership.

Throughout the autumn of 1933 he seemed poised for another major effort. To correspondents he claimed that the biography of Lenin would be his major work.[13] This type of commitment may seem odd in view of the demands of Trotsky's new political career and the immediate historical context: Hitler's rise to power and Trotsky's sense of the enormous threat posed by Nazism. But the importance of the project to Trotsky is confirmed by Natalia Sedova Trotsky, his second wife and constant companion during exile. She made "His Projected Book on Lenin" one of the subheadings of her brief reminiscences for the memorial publication issued on November 7, 1969, the ninetieth anniversary of Trotsky's birth. This, oddly enough, is also the anniversary of the October Revolution (the difference between October 25 and November 7 arising from the thirteen-day lag between the Russian Julian calendar and the Western Gregorian calendar adopted after the Revolution). Here she wrote: "It was not without sorrow that he had to renounce for the time being the continuation of his book on Lenin. His deep and burning desire was to *show* Lenin as he was in *reality* as against all those who had written about Lenin."[14] The remarks are detached from their immediate context, and it is impossible to infer from them a precise time or an immediate cause for Trotsky's abandonment of work on the project. Nonetheless, it seems hardly surprising that by the spring of 1935 Trotsky found it difficult to pour his main energies into the work on Lenin's biography. In his diary entry of April 4 he stated, "It is hard right now to work on my book on Lenin: my thoughts simply don't want to concentrate on the year 1893."[15] Trotsky never did get beyond 1893—rather, he never completed a publishable manuscript for the years after 1893—although he did leave behind uncompleted manuscripts for later years. Trot-

Lenin and Revolutionary Politics

sky finally completed only a slim volume on Lenin's youth. It was published in French in 1936 under the title *La Vie de Lenine: Jeunesse* and subsequently appeared in several languages, including English.[16]

Given Trotsky's initially strong motivation and his extraordinary ability to complete literary projects, once he put his mind to them, factors other than immediate political concerns in the period 1933–35 might also have been involved in the abandonment of the biography. An examination of Trotsky's other publications on Lenin might yield clues. Previously, Trotsky had published several sketches of Lenin at different moments of his career and most of them were collected in a volume entitled *On Lenin,* which appeared in 1924. Several of them are obviously propagandistic or sentimental.[17] The more valuable of the sketches that make up the book deal with Lenin in 1902–3, at a crucial moment in the history of Russian Marxism, and with several momentous decisions of the period 1917–20: Lenin's decision to overthrow the Provisional Government in 1917 and to dissolve the Constituent Assembly in 1918; his decision to surrender vast amounts of Soviet territory to the Germans in the treaty of Brest-Litovsk in 1918; the decision to pursue the idea of a revolutionary dictatorship without hesitation or wavering once Lenin had established his government; Lenin's decisions during the early phases of the Civil War, in the spring and summer of 1918; and the unfortunate decision to "sound . . . the situation in Poland" in 1920 when the Red Army was repulsed before Warsaw.[18] Thus, Trotsky had "covered" the periods 1870–93, 1902–3, and 1917–20 in some fashion. In the latter two periods Trotsky's own career intersected Lenin's, and the sketches have the character of reminiscences as well as installments toward a biography. They were also probably designed to reinforce Trotsky's weak standing in the Party by showing his closeness to Lenin—his partnership with him. Trotsky had, in fact, aroused the hostility of his colleagues on the Central Committee of the Party in 1924 by emphasizing his own and Lenin's role in 1917, while dredging up their mistakes and their opposition to Lenin. His long essay "Lessons of October" was especially rankling and opened a polemical struggle with the oligarchs of the Party. Trotsky continued the attack with redoubled vigor after being exiled. The exile freed him to deal with the material with even greater candor.

It is therefore not surprising that the notebooks deal with some of the gaps, particularly with the period after 1903 and before 1917. But these were the years of Trotsky's alienation from Lenin and the Bolshevik "faction," as it was called, and both the choice of notebooks and Trotsky's abandonment of the Lenin project might have been symptomatic of a feeling of diffidence issuing from Trotsky's sense of his own remoteness from that period of Lenin's career. He must have known how vulnerable his claims as a historian would be, and in this instance, rightly so, before the epigones who had joined the Bolshevik faction in those years. His lack of tenure as an old Bolshevik had had a devastating effect on his position in the party after Lenin's death. Thus, Lenin's early years, his prehistory, so to speak, belonged to no one, and Trotsky might legitimately lay claim to the years when he had been Lenin's partner in leadership, but the years in between belonged to the old Bolsheviks. Even so, it seems that Trotsky intended to show that the Bolshevik Central Committee had suffered from divisiveness in the earlier period of the party's history as well as in 1917–24. Lenin had acted without a unified committee in both that period and the later period. Trotsky's legitimacy as a Bolshevik and his claim to heirship rested to some extent upon Lenin's unsentimental and sometimes ruthless treatment of his own close colleagues. This is the apparent significance of the section in the second notebook dealing with the Moscow insurrection of 1905. But all the while, Trotsky probably felt less than enthusiastic about trying to portray Lenin during the years 1904–17.

One might even speculate that Trotsky's feeling for biography faded once his subject emerged from a subhistorical existence, as it were, into the historical world. Perhaps something like this is signified by a passage in his autobiography, *My Life,* in which he describes his arrival in Petrograd in 1917: "Immediately after the welcome at the station, I found myself in a whirlpool in which men and events swept by me as swiftly as litter on a rushing

Lenin and Revolutionary Politics

stream. The most important events are now the least charged with personal memories, for thus does memory guard against burdening itself too heavily."[19] Trotsky, of course, was quite conscious of his historiographical bias against historians who, in his view, exaggerated the role of greatness or genius in history. During the composition of *The History of the Russian Revolution* he had declared:

> Historians and biographers of the psychological tendency not infrequently seek and find something purely personal and accidental where great historical forces are refracted through a personality. . . . We do not at all pretend to deny the significance of the personal in the mechanics of the historic process, nor the significance in the personal of the accidental. We only demand that a historic personality, with all its peculiarities, should not be taken as a bare list of psychological traits, but as a living reality grown out of definite social conditions and reacting upon them. As a rose does not lose its fragrance because the natural scientist points out upon what ingredients of soil and atmosphere it is nourished, so an exposure of the social roots of a personality does not remove from it either its aroma or its foul odor.[20]

Despite his fully ripened conviction about Lenin's indispensability in October, in 1933–35 Trotsky had not abandoned his basic position as a historian—that of Marxian historical sociology, in which the leadership of the Russian Revolution had to be the product of larger social forces and class struggle. To this effect, he wrote: "The author does not feel great respect for the biographical school of historiography, E. Ludwig, Maurois, and others, who tear the individual from the milieu and [give themselves all the greater] liberty to fill up the empty space with psychological constructions."[21] All the figures in Trotsky's biographical works and sketches are connected by quite visible threads with the class struggle, with their conscious and unconscious roles in that struggle. For this reason, Trotsky had to emphasize those aspects of their personalities that crucially affected the way they played their historical roles, the qualities that gave them their strengths and weaknesses as political actors, and the connection of their willpower (or lack of it) to their class commitments.

Trotsky's contempt for the psychologizing of early psychobiographers like Emil Ludwig no doubt affected his efforts at biography and perhaps in the end prevented him from applying some of the insights of the "biographical school." Although among Russian Marxist political leaders he was unique in his appreciation for the role of unconscious factors in both personal and social history, he denied himself the license to practice psychoanalysis in his biography of Lenin. Rather, he vividly portrayed the complex relationships within the Ulianov family and their impact on the future leader of the Russian Revolution. Later biographers have been less reluctant to apply psychoanalysis to Lenin, but in doing so they have often relied upon material perceptively worked up by Trotsky.

Although contemporary radical thinkers tend to be suspicious of any intrusion of biology into historical investigation at a level lower than ecosystems, Trotsky showed keen interest in biological factors, genetic inheritances—"organic" strengths and weaknesses—in his study of Lenin. His historical materialism embraced Mendelian genetics, and in his biography of Lenin he explicitly referred to Lenin's hereditary endowment. The little section in the notebooks on genius is also instructive. Trotsky believed that Lenin had been "selected" by history. Biological gifts and Lenin's "exercise" of them played their part in the movement from the personal to the historical realm.

Trotsky's labors for his biography of Lenin were not just a pious search for the sources of the hero's greatness. This was precisely what he wanted to avoid. Personal details that lend verisimilitude to a life appear abundantly in his own autobiography and in his story of Lenin's childhood and adolescence, each work brilliant and revealing in its own way. Even in the essays on Lenin's career published in 1924 after Lenin's death, Trotsky had pointed out Lenin's poor judgment in 1920 when he decided to send the Red Army to Warsaw. Some of the speeches and articles published in 1924 might be interpreted as the most slavish and sentimental hero worship, but only if the political and ceremonial context is ignored. Here too the notebooks are useful, for they present with great clarity Trotsky's approach to a political career

Lenin and Revolutionary Politics

taken as a whole. Trotsky uses the metaphor of accounting when he measures Lenin against his opponents, and Trotsky's judgment can hardly be questioned, particularly if we remain within the interpretive boundaries set by him—taking Lenin's measure within the context of revolutionary politics and alongside his political opponents. Trotsky was also fond of metaphors associated with photography and cinematography, something to which the notebooks testify. To borrow one of his favorite images, his "snapshots" of Lenin may be carefully cropped, but they are hardly icons of the sort that were mass produced in the Soviet Union by the epigones.

Trotsky on Lenin and Stalin

During the composition of the notebooks Trotsky had reflected, no doubt with some pain, on the historical connection between Lenin and the most successful epigone, Stalin. A brief but eloquent two-sentence statement, which itself occupies an entire page of the second notebook, puts the connection rather starkly: "Lenin created the apparatus. The apparatus created Stalin." It would appear from this succinct assertion that he was on the verge of condemning Lenin for creating the conditions favoring Stalin's rise to power, but the blankness on the remainder of the page is also eloquent. Trotsky eventually wrote a vast amount trying to explain Stalin and Stalin's rise to power and found several ways to separate Leninism from Stalinism. For example, he stressed the ways in which Lenin violated his own principles of party conduct or was unable to implement them—a seemingly odd way to exculpate Lenin, but one which figures prominently in contemporary assessments of the differences between Lenin's conduct of party affairs and Stalinism.

> It is true that for fifteen years prior to the October Revolution Lenin had agitated for [a] strictly disciplined party of professional revolutionaries as the condition sine qua non for the conquest and

maintenance of power. Nevertheless, throughout his career, including the five years of his active life after the victory of October, Lenin never managed to organize such a "monolithic" party. *Nor was it ever more than a pious wish with him which he constantly violated.* Bolshevism, born of polemics and factionalism, flourished throughout the twenty years of its Leninist period on arguments and dissensions. It was only after Lenin's death, after Stalin's ruthless police measures had strangled the Bolshevik party, after the red color of pulsing life had been drained from its veins, that it assumed the rigidity of a mummified corpse; it is not impossible that it may yet turn upon its maker in the manner of Frankenstein's monster.[22]

But could Trotsky have been unaware that the notion of a Frankenstein monster might be equally apt for the relationship between Lenin and Stalin? A connection of this sort is implicit in the words "Lenin created the apparatus. The apparatus created Stalin."

Now and again Trotsky confronted another problem: Lenin's apparent admiration for and promotion of Stalin in the party. Here Trotsky showed that Lenin had indeed prized certain of Stalin's qualities and skills and had promoted him in the party because of their usefulness. But Trotsky emphasized that Lenin had never intended that Stalin play a major political role. Rather, Stalin had been a kind of troubleshooter, a hired gun—a man to be trusted with important administrative tasks and with the affairs of the party apparatus, but not with major political decisions.

> The ability to "exert pressure" was what Lenin prized so highly in Stalin. The more the state machine for "exerting pressure" gained momentum and the further the spirit of revolution was removed from the machine, the more confident Stalin felt.[23] . . .
>
> Undoubtedly he valued certain of Stalin's traits very highly, his firmness of character, his persistence, even his ruthlessness and striving, attributes indispensable in struggle and consequently at Party Headquarters. But as time went on, Stalin took increasing advantage of the opportunities his post presented for recruiting people personally devoted to him and for revenging himself upon his opponents.[24]

Lenin and Revolutionary Politics 29

Trotsky here confronted a very basic problem of revolutions, or indeed, of power politics in general—that of the hired guns usurping power. Precisely those types of political actors prized most by Lenin (the men of action, the ruthless leaders) might have a great will to power and vindictiveness when exercising it as well. Trotsky's own sense of revolution as class war and of the revolutionary party as a military body in some respects permitted him to understand Lenin's admiration for Stalin and other picaresque figures, among them S. A. Ter-Petrosyan, who appears in the notebooks as "Kamo" in the interesting diagram linking Nechaev with Lenin and Kamo.

The larger problem underlying all this is the relationship between revolutionary and political means and ends. The appearance of Nechaev in the notebooks as a composite of Lenin and Kamo reveals quite graphically the problem of means and ends.[25] Lenin's position at the top of the broken line undoubtedly signifies the theoretical guidance of the Revolution, whereas Kamo represents the simple but audacious man of action indispensable for the struggle. Kamo, in fact, "expropriated" a large amount of money for the Bolshevik cause in a daring raid on a bank convoy in Tbilisi Georgia in June 1907. It would appear from the diagram that Trotsky had a rather high opinion of Nechaev, for by linking him with Kamo rather than with Stalin he connected him with a benign type of hired gun. Trotsky's sympathetic account of Kamo's tragic career leaves little doubt that he had a positive opinion of him.[26] Yet Trotsky knew that Nechaev signified unscrupulousness, and he was aware of the opinion of Vera Zasulich, whose long revolutionary career had exposed her to both Nechaev and Lenin. She had said in an interview with a Soviet historian that she "knew Lenin well—that he is a person of the Nechaev type, unscrupulous about means in the service of revolution." Trotsky had excerpted this passage and had collected a great deal of material on Nechaev as part of his research for his biography of Lenin.[27]

In his writings Trotsky repeatedly returned to the problem of revolutionary morality. He dealt with it concisely in an elegant sentence toward the end of *The Young Lenin*: "His code of justice was the laws of struggle."[28] But during his work on Lenin's biography he was well aware that the problem demanded more attention and that Lenin had to be defended against the accusation of "Nechaevshchina." Trotsky's defense justified revolutionary terror and the use of whatever means came to hand:

> Lenin assessed people according to their relationship to the fundamental historical task and even for the immediate task ahead; he did not compose a list of their positive and negative traits and did not weigh them dispassionately; rather, he took each person on the basis of the side that faced the party, the revolution; not infrequently, he had to change his evaluation, and then he always expressed it in extreme form; he was profoundly partial. . . . This was expedient, in most instances, the fully conscious partiality of a revolutionary leader. . . .
>
> During a war the most unimpeachable officer prefers the soldier who can carry out a daring mission, even if he had been a gangster earlier. If you want to make an accusation of unscrupulousness as to means, then it shouldn't be directed against the officer, but against the war, or the regime that generated the war. During his entire life Lenin conducted warfare—not in the name of a nation, but in the name of the oppressed, in the last analysis—in the name of humanity, and he very well appreciated the sense of realism in the rule: à la guerre comme à la guerre.[29]

Trotsky's defense of Lenin, of course, is a kind of self-defense, for Trotsky too had ruthlessly used whatever means were available when conducting revolutionary war and had not flinched at the use of terror. He also felt that he had to defend the reputation of the Bolshevik Party, the historical agency of the Revolution, against the attacks of both "reactionary philistines" and the "aberrations" of Soviet historians who tried to connect Bolshevism and the Revolution with the kind of terrorism practiced by Nechaev and preached in his and Bakunin's notorious "Catechism of a Revolutionary." To do this and to show that Stalin's ruthlessness and amoralism were somehow different was not a simple matter.

Trotsky found himself in the odd position of protecting the

Lenin and Revolutionary Politics

reputations of Nechaev and Bakunin, while simultaneously rejecting their "romanticism" and "terroristic materialism."

> In the Soviet period several young historians of the revolution tried to establish a resemblance between the revolutionary catechism and the methods of Bolshevism. A linkage of this sort opens the way to nothing more than a simplistic historical aberration. Insofar as the bureaucracy separated itself from the masses, in its struggle for self-preservation it was forced increasingly to resort to the very methods of terroristic materialism, which Bakunin had recommended in the interests of holy anarchy, but which he himself rejected in a fright, when he saw them applied by Nechaev. If a few imprudent theoreticians of the Stalinist school try to shake hands with Nechaev over the head of Bolshevism, then we are prepared to protect Nechaev's ghost. That incorruptible revolutionary would reject the outstretched hand. Nechaev tried to fight for the liberation of the masses, whereas the bureaucracy struggles for their enslavement. According to Bakunin's catechism every revolutionary is doomed, whereas according to the catechism of the Soviet bureaucracy, everyone who fights against its domination is doomed.[30]

Trotsky seems to have forgotten the very deed that had inspired horror of Nechaevism among Russian revolutionaries. Nechaev had murdered a member of his organization, a "spy." Stalin, of course, practiced purging on a massive scale and with unprecedented violence, also under the pretext of meting out justice to spies and traitors. Indeed, Trotsky himself had been accused of using unnecessary violence against the Party during the Civil War.[31] Now, Trotsky in exile found himself both justifying Bolshevik ruthlessness and trying to distinguish it from Stalin's immoderate will to power. He could not accept the idea that Stalin was the logical result of Leninism or the embodiment of the Bolshevik spirit.

Trotsky's intellectual conscience was no cleaner than his political hands. As early as 1904, shortly after Lenin had precipitated the split in Russian Marxism over the organization of the Russian Social Democratic Workers' Party, Trotsky had written a pamphlet, *Our Political Tasks,* in which he had made the following prediction: "The party organization will substitute itself for the party, the central committee will substitute itself for the organization, and finally, a dictator will substitute himself for the central committee."[32] In addition, the booklet contained a savage attack upon Lenin. However, once he joined the Bolshevik Party in 1917, Trotsky had to repudiate his earlier position. Even so, he could not avoid the chronic resentment of those who had served longer in the Party but had received less glory and authority. In a way, he was the Benjamin of the Party, although he himself reserved that title for Bukharin. Thus, when Trotsky practiced ruthlessness he found himself doubly resented; and one to whom ruthlessness came naturally—Stalin—nonetheless called Trotsky a hero with fake muscles. There can be no question that Stalin considered himself to be a better Bolshevik and Lenin's legitimate heir. Trotsky in exile had to establish his own heirship and could not afford the luxury of holding up his earlier prophecy as political wisdom.

In 1939, while trying to complete his biography of Stalin and explaining to the world what had gone wrong with the Soviet Union, Trotsky acknowledged the correctness of his prediction of 1904, without endangering either Lenin's or his own legitimacy. Thus he wrote, "It is not difficult to see that these lines provide a quite precise picture of that process of degeneration which the Bolshevik party has suffered for the last fifteen years."[33] Yet he had to renounce its deeper wisdom in order to fend off the attacks of contemporary critics of Bolshevism like Boris Souvarine, who used Trotsky's booklet of 1904 against him: "Small wonder that several historians try to use this formula as proof that Stalinism was fully postulated in Lenin's methods. . . . The prognosis in my youthful pamphlet is in no way distinguished by the historical profundity which some authors groundlessly attribute to it. . . . Such generalizations can be found, not only in the pamphlet of 1904, but somewhat earlier, for example, in Plutarch, and perhaps in Thucydides."[34] Although in 1939 Trotsky still could not countenance the idea that Lenin's entire project had been misconceived and that Stalin was indeed Lenin's heir, he did confront the issue of the centralization of the Party.

Whenever Trotsky justified Lenin's organizational central-

Lenin and Revolutionary Politics

ism, he tended to invoke one of Lenin's own bits of folk wisdom: If the twig is bent, then in order to set things straight one has to bend it even farther in the other direction. The Russian revolutionary movement had suffered from organizational disunity, diffuseness, and vulnerability to infiltration by the police. Lenin had tried to fashion a secure underground party. But he had never intended to establish a monolithic centralism. Rather, he had sought political equilibrium:

> Ultimately, despite the greatest difficulties . . . upheavals . . . waverings to one side or the other, the Party sustained a necessary equilibrium of elements of both democracy and centralism. The best proof of this equilibrium is the historical fact that the Party absorbed the proletarian vanguard, that this vanguard through democratic mass organizations such as trade unions, and then soviets, was able to pull after it an entire class and even more—an entire nation of working people. This mighty historical exploit would have been impossible without a combination of the broadest democracy, which allows the expression of the feelings and thoughts of the broadest masses, with centralism—which assures firm leadership. The destruction of this equilibrium was not the logical result of Lenin's organizational principles, but the political result of a change in the correlation between party and class. The party degenerated socially—became an organization of the bureaucracy. An exaggerated centralism became essential for its self-defense. Revolutionary centralism became bureaucratic centralism; the apparatus, which, in its resolution of internal conflicts cannot and does not dare to appeal to the masses, was forced to set up a court of higher appeal above itself. Thus, bureaucratic centralism inevitably leads to personal dictatorship.[35]

With considerable rhetorical skill and adroitness at constructing historical sociologies to support his political line, Trotsky in 1939 defended Lenin's centralism against young Trotsky's prescience. The defense of Lenin was simultaneously Trotsky's self-defense and an attack upon Stalin.

Thus, the little diagram linking Nechaev with Lenin and Kamo suggests, however schematically, Trotsky's faith that if one had to bend the twig too far, then it should be to the left. The comparisons of Lenin with other political opponents, who were both to the right of Lenin and irresolute in their political behavior, complement the schema. Lenin's political achievement, his genius, and dialectics had become articles of faith for Trotsky. It seems odd, then, that in his own "Testament" of February 27, 1940, Trotsky identified himself as a proletarian revolutionist, a Marxist, and a dialectical materialist—but not as a Leninist.[36] It may be that in the end, when he had to summarize his credo and affirm his revolutionary career, Trotsky said as much by omitting Leninism as he did by leaving an eloquent blankness after the two sentences "Lenin created the apparatus. The apparatus created Stalin."

During 1933–35 Trotsky was creating an image of Lenin that would permit him to reassert his own self-transformation and acceptance of Bolshevik ruthlessness. It cannot be stressed too much that Trotsky identified himself with Lenin when he took Lenin's measure. For example, in the comparison of Lenin with Martov in the notebooks there are very clear resemblances with a passage in *My Life* in which Trotsky's intuitive decisiveness is contrasted with Martov's confusion:

> In October [1905], I plunged headlong into the gigantic whirlpool, which, in a personal sense, was the greatest test of my powers. Decisions had to be made under fire. I can't help noting that those decisions came to me quite obviously. I did not turn back to see what others might say, and I very seldom had the opportunity to consult anybody; everything had to be done in such a hurry. Later, I observed with astonishment and a sense of estrangement how every event caught the cleverest of the Mensheviks, Martov, unawares and threw him into confusion. Without thinking about it— there was too little time for self-examination—I organically felt that my years of apprenticeship were over, although not in the sense that I'd stopped learning.[37]

In *My Life* Trotsky could do for his own career what he would like to have done for Lenin's: He could portray his own feelings and even attempt to show how unconscious processes work in history—a matter which will be examined below in the discussion of the notes on dialectics. He could show that even the greatest

Lenin and Revolutionary Politics

lives, however organic and harmonious, progressed through mistakes, "breaks" (in Russian, "perelomy"), and creative breakthroughs. Indeed, Trotsky had every intention of repeating Lenin's triumphal return from emigration in April 1917, when Lenin forced the epigones in his own party to set the revolution on a true course.

Trotsky's interpretation of Lenin's larger historical role is far more vulnerable to criticism than his skillful portrayal of the young␣enin, his appreciation of Lenin as a revolutionary politician, and his assessments of Lenin's political opponents. Criticisms of Trotsky's interpretation of history and Lenin's role in it abound, as do general criticisms of Marxist historiography. There is no need to rehearse them here. The material on Lenin in the notebooks reveals the depth of Trotsky's commitment to the October Revolution, and echoes some of Trotsky's earlier positions, but there are new questions and new insights. However, no ambiguity or doubt exists in Trotsky's public assessment of Lenin. He never took back his assertion that Lenin was a political genius and a mighty link in the chain of historical progress. There can be little doubt that his affirmation of Lenin's historical role was simultaneously a form of self-affirmation. Readers may judge for themselves whether Trotsky's statements in the notebooks have an odor of incense about them.

2. Notes on Dialectics and Evolutionism

Trotsky's writings on philosophical matters constitute a very small part of his total corpus. Jean van Heijenoort, who lived with Trotsky in exile and served him as bodyguard, secretary, and translator between October 1932 and September 1936, and then again between January 1937 and November 1939, observed that Trotsky's work regimen reflected the preeminence of political concerns during these years.[1] Trotsky devoted the earlier part of the day to his work on politics, and only when he had expended the best part of his energies did he turn to other matters. This had not always been the case. Like most members of the intelligentsia Trotsky had spent many hours in his youth poring over the great socialist texts, European and Russian, and in the period 1898–1901, when in prison and internal exile, had exerted heroic autodidactic efforts to deepen and extend his knowledge. The early period is chronicled in Trotsky's autobiography and is nicely summarized in Deutscher's biography of him.[2] During the period 1922–26 Trotsky had devoted considerable time to problems of culture. *Literature and Revolution,* undoubtedly his best-known work on culture, appeared in 1923, and he wrote several essays (often delivered as speeches) on the philosophy of science and issues surrounding dialectical materialism during the mid-twenties.[3]

Trotsky's late writings on dialectical materialism are better known to the English-speaking world, for they were polemics against American dissenters from the doctrinal orthodoxy Trotsky was trying to enforce on his followers. The "letters" and essays making up the polemics of 1939–40 against, mainly, James Burnham and Max Shachtman were collected and published in 1942 in a single volume entitled *In Defense of Marxism*.[4] The polemics confirm Trotsky's deep commitment to the method of dialectical materialism and his belief that abandonment of it inevitably led to defection from the movement, but the philosophical discussion of dialectics as such is remarkably concise. Burnham, a professor of philosophy at New York University at the time of the furor, justly noted in his reply to Trotsky's "Open Letter to Comrade Burnham" (January 7, 1940) that Trotsky's discussion of logic betrayed ignorance of twentieth-century contributions to that area.[5]

Jean van Heijenoort's observation that Trotsky read very lightly and sporadically during 1932–40 in areas like philosophy and sociology is reinforced by Trotsky's own candor in his diary of 1935, where in an entry for May 16 he confesses that despite his growing interest in philosophy he has made little progress in his philosophical studies and has little hope that he will master the literature.[6] Despite the justice of the above assessments, one should make allowance for Trotsky's brilliance at grasping the essentials of an argument, position, or text after minimal acquaintance with it and his extraordinary ability to summarize and present a complex position epigrammatically. These qualities appeared very early in Trotsky's career and are attested to by the otherwise ill-intentioned memoirs of one of Trotsky's colleagues during his revolutionary apprenticeship.[7] Moreover, Trotsky tried to keep up with advancing knowledge in the natural sciences, although only as a dilettante, through articles on the natural sciences designed for nonspecialists, popular accounts of scientific discoveries in the press.[8] Finally, despite his superficial knowledge of some areas and his almost total neglect of others, very few actors fully engaged in political struggle have exhibited anything close to Trotsky's impressive combination of knowledge and talent.

Lenin's philosophical efforts were undoubtedly more impressive than Trotsky's, despite the dubious value of Lenin's ma-

Dialectics and Evolutionism 39

jor work, *Materialism and Empirio-Criticism,* and the mainly biographical significance (for Lenin's intellectual biography, that is) of his voluminous *Philosophical Notebooks.* Lenin's scouring of philosophical materials, evidenced by his characteristically thorough note-taking and numerous marginal comments in texts, was not altogether alien to Trotsky. His books too contain numerous underlinings and marginal notes, but unlike Lenin he did not make a habit of keeping notebooks on philosophical works. Perhaps he was inspired by a reading of Lenin's philosophical notebooks, which were first published in 1929–31 in *Leninskii sbornik,* a multivolume serial devoted to the publication of Lenin's writings. Trotsky had almost a full run of the serial and possessed Lenin's notebooks among the volumes he had with him in exile.[9] Trotsky might even have imitated (whether consciously or unconsciously) some of Lenin's distinctive multilingual annotations when he began his own notebook on Hegel.[10] It is clear from the scantiness of his notes that he quickly abandoned any effort to deal exhaustively with Hegel's *Wissenschaft der Logik* or to produce voluminous, Leninlike excerpts and annotations.[11]

Trotsky's impatience with philosophical texts and his preference for conciseness in philosophical discourse, well illustrated by his admiration for Antonio Labriola's *Essays on the Materialistic Conception of History,* shed a great deal of light on the character of the notebooks of 1933–35 which, in the absence of future discoveries, contain Trotsky's most interesting observations on dialectics and, more than any other writings, reveal his style as a dialectician.[12] One might, therefore, pause to ask why the notebooks have been passed over by students of Trotsky.

The character of the two notebooks, one of which contains only a few handwritten pages and both of which are written mainly in pencil in a somewhat careless scrawl, probably signaled to most researchers that there was little of significance in them. Furthermore, they are interfiled with the material that Trotsky was collecting during 1933–35 for his planned biography of Lenin, which, as noted above, he intended to be a magnum opus. Given the unprepossessing physical appearance of the notebooks, earlier researchers probably believed that the materials in them were too fragmentary to be of much value, or perhaps merely notes ancillary to the work on Lenin, which Trotsky never completed. Although the latter assumption is substantially correct, the notes on dialectics are sufficiently coherent to establish Trotsky's position on dialectics and permit us to speculate about the connection between that distinctive position and Trotsky's revolutionary career.

Trotsky's distinguished biographer, Isaac Deutscher, evidently belonged to the category of those who dismissed the notebooks as part of the abandoned biography of Lenin. In the course of discussing Trotsky's research for the biography of Lenin, Deutscher asserted, "Preparing to deal with Lenin's philosophical writings and conscious of gaps in his own knowledge, he went back to the classics of logic and dialectics, Aristotle and Descartes, but especially Hegel."[13] This is all that Deutscher had to say on the subject, and what he does say betrays ignorance of the contents of the notebooks. Baruch Knei-Paz, a careful student of Trotsky's thought, in his recent book, *The Social and Political Thought of Leon Trotsky,* which contains a section on Trotsky's philosophical thought as well, refers to the entry for May 16 in Trotsky's diary for 1935, mentioned above. Trotsky recorded that he had just "written a little about the interrelationship between the physiological determinism of brain processes and the 'autonomy' of thought, which is subject to the laws of logic."[14] Knei-Paz went on to say that the "essay" had apparently not been preserved.[15] However, it is clear from a comparison of this brief description with the material on the last leaves of the second notebook and from the reference to Fritz Wittels' book on Freud both in the diary entry and the last part of the notebook that Trotsky was referring to the notebook. And it also seems that Trotsky, with his diary entry, was declaring his abandonment of the project, for he added, "My philosophical interests have been growing during recent years, but, alas, [my] knowledge is too inadequate and too little time remains for a large and serious work."[16] We thus can establish May 16, 1935, as the precise date when he halted work on the second, and last, notebook on dialectics. Other scattered notes on dialectics on slips of paper are

Dialectics and Evolutionism

filed among Trotsky's materials for his book on Lenin, but nothing like a systematic project developed. The project on dialectics ancillary to the book on Lenin suffered the same fate as the book itself. Trotsky never completed it.

It is impossible to establish precisely the day or even the month when Trotsky began the notes on Hegel and dialectics, but he wrote "1933-1934" on the first page of the second notebook, and his correspondence permits us to establish roughly the autumn of 1933 as the beginning point for the first notebook. The entry of May 16, 1935, of course, invalidates Trotsky's own dating on the first page of the second notebook, but he evidently added the last entry after a final inspiration—perhaps that of Wittels' book on Freud.[17] In the remainder of this essay, the following will be attempted: an explication of Trotsky's motives for writing the notebooks; the connection of the positions taken in the notebooks with those taken in earlier writings on the same subjects; an analysis of Trotsky's style as a dialectician by way of a brief comparison with Lenin's and Bukharin's dialectical styles; an analysis of Trotsky's dialectics in the light of revealing passages in his autobiography; and a brief speculation about the direction Trotsky might have taken had he developed the ideas in the notebooks more fully.

The Motive: The Controversy with Max Eastman

It is not difficult to establish Trotsky's motives for beginning the notebooks. The notebooks were indeed connected with Trotsky's projected biography of Lenin, but the immediate stimulus came from a quarrel with Max Eastman over dialectical method.[18] The doctrinally volatile American man of letters, whose efforts to add Dewey and to subtract dialectics from "scientific socialism" immediately got him into trouble with Trotsky, refused to be ignored. Trotsky had initially turned his back on Eastman's attack on dialectics in the latter's book *Marx and Lenin: The Science of Revolution,* first published in 1927. Eastman tried to draw

Trotsky out in correspondence but failed to get him to engage in a genuine intellectual exchange.[19] Rather, in 1929 Trotsky wrote Eastman that he knew of no case in thirty years in which an opponent of dialectical materialism had sustained a revolutionary commitment. Eastman replied to the effect that advances in the science of psychology, namely Freudian psychoanalysis, had changed matters.[20] In his book, Eastman had unmasked dialectics as a form of animism, a position which he might have based upon *Totem and Taboo,* in which Freud devoted a chapter entitled "Animism, Magic, and the Omnipotence of Thought" to animism and related matters. Here Freud examined a particular form of anthropomorphism, the earliest known form of spirituality in the history of religion. During this phase of human development, human mental attributes or processes were transposed to nature as spiritual forces and beings. Furthermore, Freud believed that animistic tendencies persisted in our languages, systems of belief, and philosophies despite great advances in knowledge.

Eastman took Freud's position and turned it into an attack upon the source of dialectics:

> In primitive culture it is possible to distinguish two quite different kinds of thinking—animistic thinking, in which one tries to adjust oneself to the external world as to a person, and the ordinary practical thinking by which the daily arts of life are carried on. Animistic thinking consists essentially in trying by some sort of hocus-pocus to transfer your own wishes into the external world, and so get them realized. . . . German philosophy is the ultimate grandiose convulsion of animistic thought, expiring under the encroachments of the scientific point of view. . . . Declaring that the specific motion of your mind, guided by Hegel among the logical categories, is the universal self-active motion of those categories, and this motion is the spirit of God in a process of self-contradiction and development, Hegel succeeded in converting logic itself, the very technique of science into theology.[21]

Eastman believed that one had to purge socialism of dialectics and to combine Marx and Lenin with Freud, Darwin, and Dewey in order to arrive at a true relationship to the external world, an

Dialectics and Evolutionism 43

attitude that would permit the revolutionary to be a successful engineer of the social world.

But Eastman also recognized that dialectics played a positive role for some revolutionaries in the Marxian tradition and found a psychological explanation for their success. He acknowledged the benefits of dialectics for Lenin in the following passage:

> Lenin was perhaps the most effective political thinker in history, and he was one of the most adroit. And Lenin believed that his thinking was 'dialectic'; he cultivated his mind in the shadow of this belief. There must be some value in dialectical thinking, then, besides ceremonial communion with a God of change. And indeed there is a value—not in dialectical thinking, for that does not exist—but *believing that you think dialectically.* And this value, instead of being in conflict with what I have said, is exactly the proof of it. Believing in dialectic thinking is a method by which having made false intellectualistic assumptions about the nature of thought, you can escape from them, and win back your freedom to use thought as it was meant to be used.
>
> If you know in the first place that thought is purposive, and that logical concepts and all fixed principles are but instruments of action, then you are free to think practically in a changing situation. You are free from the domination of fixed ideas. You know that purpose alone should dominate, and that ideas must always give way before facts, and you know that you must continually recur to the facts, and be ready to remodel your ideas to meet any unanticipated factual development. . . . The dialectical method with Lenin was simply a declaration of independence from the domination of fixed concepts. It was a metaphysical contraption by which he managed to defend his right to use thoughts naturally, in spite of an unnatural conception of what thoughts are.[22]

And after quoting Lenin on dialectics Eastman wrote: "That is what dialectical thinking meant to Lenin. It meant *flexibility*—a maximum of flexibility, as opposed to the 'pedantry' of ordinary intellectualism. It meant that ideas should be handled as instruments of action, and not actions mechanically deduced from ideas."[23] In short, Eastman tried to show that dialectics reflected a primitive religious mentality rather than a progressive scientific one. He believed that he was making a revolutionary revision of

Marx, that he sought only "to clear out of this revolutionary science the last vestiges of the influences of Marx's bourgeois philosophy teacher."[24] Finally, Eastman wrote to Trotsky, "It is the only form in which Marxism will ever take root in the Anglo-Saxon intelligence—of that I feel sure."[25] Statements of this sort only provoked Trotsky, as is clear from his ironic comments on the Anglo-Saxon mind in the notebooks as well as in published works.[26]

Instead of being put off by Trotsky's rejection, Eastman decided to seize the first opportunity to make his case. The opportunity came in 1932 when Trotsky invited Eastman to Prinkipo, the Turkish island on which Trotsky was temporarily bound in exile. In spite of the dispute over dialectics, the Eastman-Trotsky collaboration had continued. Eastman worked on the translation of Trotsky's *History of the Russian Revolution* and served as his literary agent. According to the account in Eastman's memoirs, he and his wife Elena stayed on Prinkipo for twelve days (July 7–18, 1932), and he claims that the account is based upon impressions written down in two installments, on July 10 and then July 18, during and immediately after the events, rather than in 1959, when the memoirs were published.[27] Whatever the value of some of Eastman's observations, the account vividly portrays the emotional charge behind Trotsky's commitment to dialectics.

> Like many great men I have met he does not seem altogether robust. There is apt to be a frailty associated with great intellect. At any rate, Trotsky, especially in our heated arguments concerning the 'dialectic,' in which he becomes excited and wrathful to the point of losing his breath, seems to me at times almost weak. He seems too small for the struggle. He cannot laugh at my attacks on his philosophy, or be curious about them—as I imagine Lenin would—because in that field he is not secure. He is not strongly based. . . . Yesterday we reached a point of tension in our argument about dialectic that was extreme. Trotsky's throat was throbbing and his face was red; he was in a rage.[28]

Eastman then describes how the argument broke off and they returned to their work on the translation.

But Eastman was a persistent man and tried once again in

Dialectics and Evolutionism   45

the summer of 1933, after Trotsky's resettlement in France, to engage him in an epistolary exchange on dialectics. Trotsky replied on November 6, 1933. The letter is friendly in tone and praises Eastman for the manuscript "Arts and Letters under Stalin," which Eastman had sent several weeks earlier, but it goes on to repeat Trotsky's earlier position on dialectics:

> I wrote to you some time ago, that I didn't know of a single case, when a disagreement in the area of philosophy (more precisely, epistemology and method) did not lead to political disagreements. . . . I am starting a book on Lenin. In this book I hope to make a statement about dialectical materialism in a positive and critical form. In the appendix to the book I will try to evaluate the views in this area. That is why I am declining polemics of a partisan character. . . . I will devote all of the next year to the book on Lenin.[29]

Eastman adds confirmation in a footnote to his book *Stalin's Russia and the Crisis in Socialism,* published in 1940: "Trotsky has steadfastly threatened to devote an appendix in his Life of Lenin to my theoretic annihilation. I suppose I am now saving him the trouble. He will dismiss me, in the light of this book, by 'administrative decree.' "[30]

The correspondence with Eastman and references to him in the notebooks (as well as scattered attacks on him in other correspondence and in print) suggest that Eastman's critique of dialectics and his effort to be a kind of gadfly did succeed.[31] Trotsky was provoked into a reply but, contrary to Eastman's somewhat self-centered interpretation of his motives, wanted to make it his own statement about dialectics rather than a mere attack upon Eastman's views. Despite Trotsky's abandonment of the project in 1935, he later used some of the ideas in 1939–40 when Burnham and Shachtman replaced Eastman as his major doctrinal antagonists within his own movement. However, the later polemics do not have the same qualities of open-minded inquiry as the notebooks, and Trotsky seemed to be content to use heavy irony and formulaic statements about dialectics as bludgeons against his opponents.

The Themes of the Earlier Period and the Notebooks

One is immediately struck by the way in which Trotsky brought Darwin and evolutionism into his most thoughtful writings on dialectical issues. Discussions of Darwinism were part of the education of any young Russian *intelligent,* but Trotsky's recollections of his youthful response to Darwin and his later writings suggest an impact no less than that of Marx. When as a still worshipful disciple of Darwin, Trotsky had first encountered Eastman in the period 1922–24 and given him materials toward a biography, he had written:

> Darwin stood for me like a mighty doorkeeper at the entrance to the temple of the universe. I was intoxicated with his minute, precise, conscientious, and at the same time powerful, thought. I was the more astonished when I read in one of the books of Darwin, his autobiography, I think, that he had preserved his belief in God. I absolutely declined to understand how a theory of the origin of species by way of natural and sexual selection, and a belief in God, could find room in one and the same head. . . . That is the most I can tell you about my stay in the Odessa prison.[32]

Trotsky's interest in Darwin and evolutionism never abated, which is clear from the notebooks and scattered notes in the archives. Trotsky published an article on Darwinism in 1901 during his first period of internal exile. The article, entitled "A Russian Darwin," ridiculed the ideas of one Timofei Petrovich Solov'ev. Ironically enough, Trotsky chastised Solov'ev for engaging in animism (without using the term). In the course of his attack Trotsky wrote, "The philosopher subjugates lifeless nature to the spirit, injecting into it the entire guidance system in his brain corresponding to a series of ideas which inspire him, that is, in so many words he assuredly makes nature 'work.' "[33] The young Trotsky understood anthropomorphism—animism—yet the aging exile found himself accused of it. Eastman therefore stood to Trotsky in the same relationship that Trotsky stood to Darwin when he expressed astonishment at Darwin's belief in God. Each man believed he might rescue the object of his admiration by separating the sci-

Dialectics and Evolutionism 47

entific and progressive aspects of his doctrine from a heritage of illusions and personal weaknesses.

Finally, one should note that Trotsky at the time when he was writing the notebooks fully appreciated the role of Darwinism in his own spiritual life. Darwinian evolution was so central to his total world view that he found it difficult to separate dialectics from it. Many of the notes in the archives entitled "Dialektika" are about Darwinian evolution. Trotsky also often kept excerpts from other writers among his own notes. One such excerpt with the same title is from the correspondence of G. V. Plekhanov and P. B. Aksel'rod, a letter from Aksel'rod dated February 16, 1898. Aksel'rod wrote about his own spiritual needs, almost apologetically, and ended: "If there is no god, creator of the universe—and praise be to him, that he does not exist, for at least we can cut off the heads of Tsars, but wouldn't be able to do anything against a despotic Jehovah—then let us prepare the way for the appearance of a breed of earthly gods, beings with all-powerful reason and will, who enjoy both consciousness and self-consciousness, and are capable of embracing the world and ruling it by means of thought—here is the psychological basis of all my spiritual and social yearnings, designs, and actions. . . . At the beginning of the seventies [1870s] I drew (yes, and even now, sinner that I am, still draw) nourishment for this, my 'faith' in darwinism."[34] Aksel'rod had played a significant role in Trotsky's spiritual development during the latter's first European exile, and a certain resemblance can be seen between Trotsky's "Testament" and Aksel'rod's letter. There can be no doubting the integration of Darwinism with dialectics in Trotsky's thought.

Trotsky's appreciation for Darwinian theory appears in a new light in an essay on Karl Kautsky, which he began in 1919 but did not publish until 1922. Here Trotsky exhibited a characteristically revolutionary approach to evolutionary theory, an approach, one might add, that has been revived by contemporary biologists. This is the relevant passage:

> The Darwinian theory of the origin of species encompasses the entire span of development of the plant and animal kingdoms.

The struggle for survival and the processes of natural and sexual selection proceed continuously and uninterruptedly. But if one could observe these processes with ample time at one's disposal—a millennium, say, as the smallest unit of measure—one would undoubtedly discover with one's own eyes that there are long ages of relative equilibrium in the world of living things, when the laws of selection operate almost imperceptibly, and the different species remain relatively stable, seeming the very embodiment of Plato's ideal types. But there are also ages when the equilibrium between plants, animals, and their geophysical environment is disrupted, epochs of geobiological crisis, when the laws of natural selection come to the fore in all their ferocity, and evolution passes over the corpses of entire plant and animal species. On this gigantic scale Darwinian theory stands out above all as the theory of critical epochs in plant and animal development.[35]

Although Trotsky's views in this passage seem quite precocious, they were not that unusual for Russian revolutionaries. For Bukharin, for example, recognition of the dialectical law of the transition from quantity into quality, a transition characterized by an interruption of a gradual evolutionary process and by a sudden leap to a new state of the phenomenon, was a token of a revolutionary, Marxian vision of nature and society: "Sudden leaps are often found in nature, and the notion that nature permits of no such violent alterations is merely a reflection of the fear of such shifts in society, *i.e.*, of the fear of revolution. . . . The contradictory nature of evolution, the question of cataclysmic changes, is one of the most essential theoretical questions."[36]

To return to Trotsky, in the passage following his remarks on Darwinian theory, he did indeed turn to society, but he presented his position most succinctly in a speech of June 18, 1923: "In a broad materialistic and dialectical sense Marxism is the application of Darwinism to human society. . . . Only the inner tie of Marxism and Darwinism permits us to understand the living current of being and its primal tie with inorganic nature."[37] The law of the transition from quantity into quality quite clearly signified commitment to the progressive character of catastrophic change in both nature and society for Trotsky.[38]

Dialectics and Evolutionism 49

Trotsky's efforts to translate the achievements of ideologically retrograde scientific geniuses, both Russian and non-Russian, into dialectical materialism forced him to confront the issue of scientific creativity itself. It was one thing to attack bourgeois philosophers and sociologists who could not accept dialectics, but it was quite another matter when heroes of science took ideological positions hostile to Marxism. Trotsky had several goals in mind when he wrote *Literature and Revolution* and delivered several speeches on scientific and technical topics in the period 1923–26. He wanted to make bourgeois cultural achievements available for a proletarian society, to show that hard work was essential for scientific creativity, and most important, to show that the work of great men of science did not contradict a dialectical and materialist world view but rather reinforced it.

Aside from Darwin, Trotsky rescued Mendeleev, the great Russian chemist who had formulated the periodic table of elements, Pavlov, the brilliant physiologist, and Freud, the founder of a method of psychological investigation seemingly antithetical to Pavlov's. In a letter to Pavlov dated September 27, 1923, and in several other speeches Trotsky tried to reconcile Pavlovian and Freudian methods by comparing Pavlov to a man working from the bottom of a well to make his discoveries and Freud to someone peering into the well from above.[39] Both of them, however, were materialists and started from the assumption that psychological phenomena issued from organic, physiological ones. In a speech delivered on March 1, 1926, Trotsky tried to show that Pavlov's method had limitations that Freud's method might remedy. Pavlov measured the accumulation of physiological quantities and tried to infer from it a new "psychological quality." But could one really arrive at knowledge of the sources of human poetry by studying the saliva of dogs? Trotsky took a nonreductionist position that permitted him to appreciate the autonomy of psychic processes and the value of Freud's hermeneutic approach to them.[40]

Trotsky's most significant contribution to the philosophy on science and the work that most clearly prefigures the position on dialectics which he took in the notebooks of 1933–35 is his speech "Mendeleev and Marxism," delivered on September 17,

1925.[41] It adds another dimension to his interpretation of Darwinism and presents his views on dialectics and scientific creativity in a very revealing fashion. Furthermore, Trotsky offered this essay to his followers as late as 1938 as a statement of his position on the relationship of the natural and social sciences.[42] It is his definitive published statement in the area of the philosophy of science.[43] In short, it is the source which best establishes the *continuity* of Trotsky's position from the mid-twenties until his death in 1940. "Mendeleev and Marxism" reveals both the centrality of the law of the transition from quantity into quality in his understanding of dialectics and his dialectical approach to human creativity.

Trotsky delivered his speech shortly after David Riazanov published Engels' *Naturdialektik* as the second book of the *Archive of K. Marx and F. Engels*. In the published version of the speech Trotsky cited Engels' essay entitled "The General Character of the Dialectic as Science" ("Allgemeine Natur der Dialektik als Wissenschaft").[44] In fact, the only law of dialectics that Engels illustrated in the sketch was the law of the transition of quantity into quality, even though he began the essay by specifying all three dialectical laws (in the following order): the law of the transition of quantity into quality, and the reverse; the law of the mutual interpenetration of opposites; and the law of the negation of the negation. However, as is suggested by the catastrophic approach to Darwinism displayed in Trotsky's essay on Kautsky of 1922, the publication of *Naturdialektik* probably only strengthened Trotsky's emphasis upon the "first" law of dialectics. In society as well as in nature, he believed that periods of relative equilibrium, of slow evolutionary change, gave way to epochs of violent change—to class struggle and civil war.

Perhaps the best illustration of Trotsky's use of the dialectical law of the transition from quantity into quality appears in the third volume of *The History of the Russian Revolution,* written approximately seven years after "Mendeleev and Marxism."

> Armed insurrection stands in the same relation to revolution that revolution as a whole does to evolution. It is the critical point

Dialectics and Evolutionism 51

> when accumulating quantity turns with an explosion into quality. But insurrection itself again is not a homogeneous and indivisible act: it too has its critical points, its inner crises and accelerations.
>
> An extraordinary importance both political and theoretical attaches to that short period immediately preceding the "boiling point"—the eve, that is, of the insurrection. Physics teaches that the steady increase of temperature suddenly comes to a stop; the liquid remains for a time at the same temperature, and boils only after absorbing an additional quantity of heat. Everyday language comes to our aid here, designating this condition of pseudo-tranquil concentration preceding an explosion as "the lull before the storm."[45]

However, in 1925 Trotsky showed awareness of the difficulties of comparing natural processes to social ones. Marx himself had accused Darwin of transposing to nature the struggle for existence in the social order of bourgeois England and had condemned the Malthusian elements in Darwinism: Even Darwin was guilty of the sin of anthropomorphism. Trotsky also found Darwin guilty of transposing features taken from the natural world to society. He forgave Darwin this sin too. Like Marx before him, Trotsky distinguished the dialectically progressive side of Darwin from his less enlightened side.

> This brilliant biologist, while showing how small quantitative deviations accumulate and yield a completely new biological 'quality,' in this way explaining the origin of species, applied without being conscious of it, the methods of dialectical materialism in the area of organic life. The Hegelian law of the transition from quantity into quality found in Darwin a brilliant, although philosophically unenlightened application. At the same time we frequently find in Darwin himself, not to speak of the Darwinists, completely naive and unscientific efforts to carry over the conclusions of biology to society. Interpreting competition as a 'variety' of biological struggle for existence—is like seeing nothing but mechanics in the physiology of mating.[46]

Trotsky had attacked Social Darwinism in 1923 in the speech cited earlier: "You know that there were liberal, Manchesterist efforts at a mechanical application of Darwinism to sociology, which yielded only childish analogies, covering up the malicious bourgeois apologetics: market competition proved to be an 'eternal' law of the struggle for existence, etc."[47]

All the above points up Trotsky's belief that it was possible to connect natural evolution wih social change through dialectics, and his efforts to avoid the dangers of reductionism, anthropomorphism, and false analogies. The essay of 1925 on Mendeleev adds a new idea, the idea that a great thinker might be an *unconscious dialectician*. Trotsky encountered this idea in Engels, who had applied it to Mendeleev in the essay in *Naturdialektik* already cited. In the notebooks, written almost thirty years after the first edition of *Naturdialektik*, he still found apt Engels' comparison of unconscious dialecticians like Mendeleev with Molière's Monsieur Jourdain, the man who spoke prose all his life without knowing it.[48] In the case of Mendeleev, he simply followed the lead of Engels, who had presented Mendeleev's periodic table of elements as an example of an unconscious application of the law of the transition of quantity into quality in chemistry.[49]

Engels thus provided Trotsky with a key which permitted him to appropriate ideologically retrograde scientists for the new society and its scientific culture. Trotsky had a practical motive. While explicating heroes of science and revealing them to be unconscious dialecticians, he was also promoting the value of the painstaking work, the laborious accumulation of data that lay behind scientific breakthroughs. In a speech delivered on February 3, 1926, entitled "Culture and Socialism," he asserted:

> You can't just foist dialectics on facts, but must derive it from the facts, from their nature and their development. Only painstaking work over an immense quantity of material permitted Marx to erect the dialectical system of the economy on an understanding of value as social labor. . . . To apply dialectical materialism to new areas of knowledge is possible only when you have mastered them from within. The purification of bourgeois science presupposes the mastery of bourgeois science.[50]

Marx, a conscious dialectician, had labored no less than bourgeois scientists who were unconscious dialecticians and had taken from them whatever useful they had to give.

But a deeper issue lay behind the practical concern with the promotion of scientific labor. The nature of scientific creativity was somehow connected with the law of the transition from quantity into quality in Trotsky's writing. He tried not only to understand individual creativity but to interpret scientific revolutions in the light of dialectics. In both cases, he showed that leaps and reversals were the rule, and emphasized the impatience of dialectics with boundaries and limits.

> Some objects (phenomena) are confined easily within boundaries according to logical classification, others present [us with] difficulties: they can be put here or there, but within a stricter relationship—nowhere. While provoking the indignation of systematizers, such transitional forms are exceptionally interesting to dialecticians, for they smash the limited boundaries of classification, revealing the real connections and consecutiveness of a living process.[51]

Whenever such issues arose, the law of the transition from quantity into quality soon appeared. Trotsky stated his position clearly and in his own italics: "*It must be recognized that the fundamental law of dialectics is the conversion of quantity into quality,* for it gives [us] the general formula of all evolutionary processes—of nature as well as of society."[52] Trotsky went on to say that "Hegel himself undoubtedly did not give the law of the transition of quantity into quality the paramount importance which it fully deserves."[53] Undoubtedly, Trotsky saw leaps, reversals, and the transgression of boundaries at the very heart of creativity. He had great fun with the idea of the Anglo-Saxon empiricistic mentality being constructed according to the system of the impermeable bulkhead and then extended the insult to the "average scholar," who fails to pose "those questions which issue from the *general* movement of scientific thought, and cravenly ceases to draw general conclusions when they call for a dialectical leap."[54] He extolled the virtues of the painstaking scholar, of the laborious accumulator of facts and good observations, yet admired above all the creative thinker whose "elasticity arms him with invaluable analogies and educates him in a spirit of daring, grounded in circumspection."[55]

Trotsky was undoubtedly describing himself and his own creative strengths in such passages. What he failed to notice was his continual sliding into an animistic, and therefore anthropomorphic, vision of nature and history. He was transposing those creative qualities which he sensed and admired in himself and others to the dialectics of nature and history, just as Hegel before him had projected an intuitive developmental psychology onto the Absolute Spirit in *The Phenomenology of Mind*. Despite his astuteness at picking out the anthropomorphic fallacies and doubtful analogies in others, Trotsky was blind to his own. Thus, he infused nature with a creative impulse:

> Then life creates its own banks for itself in order to wash them away. The quantitative changes of matter at a given stage push against those congealed forms, which sufficed for its previous state. Conflict, catastrophe. Either the old form conquers (only partially conquers), necessitating the self-adaptation of the conquered (partially) process, or the process of movement explodes the old form and creates a new one, by way of its new crystallizations from its wombs and the assimilation of elements of the old form.[56]

But in the course of his inquiry, Trotsky with admirable intellectual honesty began to attack problems of consciousness and cognition that in turn forced him to confront epistemological and ontological issues in greater depth. Here we see a brilliant mind at work trying to understand the mysteries of human creativity and the mystery of the evolution of human consciousness itself. In the end, he found himself reflecting upon the mind-body problem and Freud's theory of the unconscious. But it is best to set aside Freud and the unconscious until the end, and return to the problem of dialectics and creativity. Trotsky's lifelong pride in his own intellectual achievement and his creative powers became transferred, to some extent, to Lenin. His appreciation for Lenin's strengths as a dialectician yielded the interesting comparison with Martov in the notebooks, and is a convenient introduction to the problem of dialectical styles.

Dialectical Styles: Trotsky's Analysis

Trotsky introduced the issue of dialectical styles in a rather easy form—the notion that dialecticians might work on different scales and that their visions might be connected with their positions in a dialectic of social forces. In short, Trotsky applied Marxian theory in the form of the sociology of knowledge to dialectical styles and showed how they were related to social and political theory and practice. In view of the disagreements among Marxists, particularly the bitter disputes of Mensheviks and Bolsheviks, one could hardly fail to notice that dialecticians differed. Trotsky also extended his idea that dialectics might operate at an unconscious level. Not only great scientists but all modern human beings were affected by changing knowledge and a changing milieu. Indeed, all contemporary thought showed "elements" of the dialectic, something even truer for earlier schools of Marxism which had failed, in the end, to grasp the correlation of forces in the social world. They had failed because they had been adapted to "derivative processes" and operated on too small a scale. This was true of Martov, whose dialectic reflected the influence of an intelligentsia milieu and its offshoot—the workers' intelligentsia.

Trotsky suggests here that the limits of a dialectical style in politics are determined by the limited aspirations and visions of the social groups to which the dialectician is bound. Thus, Lenin, who truly represented the revolutionary proletariat, operated with a dialectic of "massive character." Of course, Trotsky was also talking about himself in the following passage:

> Lenin's thought operated with living classes as the basic factors of society and thus revealed *all* its power in those periods when the great masses entered the scene, that is, in periods of profound upheavals, wars, and revolutions. The Leninist dialectic was a dialectic for the large scale. . . . Martov's thought was the thought of a watchmaker in politics. Lenin's thought worked on the scale of Dnepostroi. . . . The politics of a minor scale . . . maintains its relative independence while the (relatively) large factors, that is, classes, are unchanging. Martov's dialectic therefore yielded the more tragic misfirings in matters of a minor scale as

well, the closer the approach of stormy class conflicts, of perturbations in the life of society. . . . To the contrary, Lenin's thought analyzed all the secondary phenomena, all the elements of the superstructure more penetratingly, the more immediately they depended upon the class movements that were occurring. From stage to stage Lenin's thought became stronger, more courageous, and at the same time subtler and more flexible.[57]

Although much of the above sounds like hero-worship and, if the surmise that Trotsky fully identified himself with the description of Lenin is correct, reveals a perhaps excessive amount of self-esteem, Trotsky knew very well that both Lenin and he tended to be deviationists of the left in revolutionary politics. He admitted that Lenin had made political mistakes, just as he admitted to his own. Thus, even dialecticians who were well connected with the revolutionary masses might err. But those who erred on the right in epochs of revolutionary upheaval had their mistakes magnified, whereas those who erred on the left found that historical developments tended to rectify their errors.

Trotsky's descriptions of two revolutionary styles and his sociohistorical explanation for them only captures some aspects of dialectical style: scale and political tendency. However, these surely do not exhaust all the dimensions of a notion of dialectical style, any more than perspective and color exhaust all aspects of a style in painting. In order to proceed further in an analysis of dialectical styles, it is necessary to step outside the limits of Trotsky's own analysis.

Dialectical Styles: Architectonics

Human creativity defies efforts at exhaustive description; so too styles in any area of human creativity discourage simple analytical approaches. Yet it is possible to detect structural principles, or architectonics, in many kinds of creative works, including philosophical ones. These are not the structures which we can abstract from the composition, but rather the structural principles

Dialectics and Evolutionism 57

employed by creative thinkers in several fields in their efforts to give shape to an imaginatively constructed and systematized unity or whole, such as nature or history. When Hegel and Engels, for example, apply a dialectical architectonic to nature and history, they express their sense of structure and motion in the language of logic rather than in the common language or mathematical languages which we ordinarily use when we describe the static and dynamic features of systemic unities. The issues underlying the use of such language are too complex to deal with here, but it is clear that dialecticians seek to give structure to both continuity and change by using terms like "thesis," "antithesis," "positive," and "negative" in ways that permit translations into the ordinary language of form, relationship, continuity, and change, or into mathematical languages. Both Hegel and Engels, for example, made such translations when they illustrated the laws of dialectics. The illustrations are familiar to students of the classics of dialectics and need not be reproduced here.[58] Suffice it to say, whether they remain within the traditional logical idiom of dialectics introduced by Hegel or use some other idiom, when dialecticians try to describe relationship, continuity, and change in systemic wholes, they unfailingly use a small number of architectonics. The term "dialectics" in ordinary usage embraces all of them, even though it is possible to identify in any given work of dialectics an emphasis upon one or another architectonic.

The emphasis of the dialectical architectonic proper, so to speak, is that of conflict or opposition, and it is impossible to conceive of a dialectical approach without a dynamic principle of *conflict*. But this by no means exhausts the structural features of dialectics as it has been used. A dialectical approach also implies a *systemic* principle, the idea of a self-generating and self-developing superordinate whole with subordinate parts; and an *epigenetic* principle, which governs development and assures the transmission of progressive elements from stage to stage of the developing system through *Aufhebung* (sublation). Marx, for example, treated each great historical epoch systematically. Each stage had its own systemic relationships which, driven by the dialectical principle, reached a point of ultimate crisis. At this point a fourth architectonic, the idea of discontinuous change, or a *catastrophic* principle, governs. It ushers in a new system, a new whole with its own laws and conflicts. Underlying some varieties of dialectical thought particularly strongly infused with mythopoeic inspiration is a *genetic* principle as well. It governs something like a return to benign origins, which occurs only at an advanced stage, when a progressively realized undifferentiated unity is finally achieved. However, the mystique of the power of origins and a sense of the goodness of the past associated with origins myths, the traditional vehicles of the genetic architectonic, have generally given way to an epigenetic vision governed by the power of the future to reshape and improve endlessly what has been transmitted from the past.

To students of dialectics, all the above is quite elementary, but the vocabulary of architectonics is a convenient way to distinguish dialectical styles, and it could not be introduced easily without some basic illustrations. Thus, it is immediately clear that Trotsky emphasized the *catastrophic* principle both in his early works and in the notebooks. It was his key signature or his dominant color as a dialectician. There are, of course, other ways to distinguish dialectical styles. Trotsky distinguished Martov from Lenin using his own principles in the example given earlier. One might distinguish dialecticians as well by the metaphors connected to their architectonics; a creative mind can manipulate metaphors with great virtuosity. For example, differences exist between closed mechanical systems and open organic ones. Systemic visions and allied metaphors offer wide latitude for diagnosis, prescription, and prediction. In addition, it is possible to emphasize in one's dialectical vision the *optimal state of the system* rather than, say, the moment of crisis and catastrophe which ushers in a leap to a new and higher stage. Quite clearly, the differences in emphasis have very serious implications. Choices of governing metaphor and distinctions in emphasis not only created differences of style among revolutionary dialecticians. They also signified differing interpretations of the historical moment, of the correlation of forces in society, and caused splits within parties governed by dialectical visions.

Dialectics and Evolutionism 59

A brief analysis of Bukharin's dialectical style might clarify the peculiarities of Trotsky's. In his major work on dialectical materialism, *Historical Materialism,* Bukharin revealed throughout that his dialectic was governed by a systemic architectonic. He continually emphasized the state of the social system and even structured his work according to the systemic idea of *equilibrium.*[59] The following, for example, is Bukharin's translation of the dialectical triad of thesis, antithesis, and synthesis into systemic terms:

> In other words, the world consists of forces, acting many ways, opposing each other. These forces are balanced for a moment in exceptional cases only. We then have a state of 'rest,' *i.e.,* their actual 'conflict' is concealed. But if we change only one of these forces, immediately the 'internal contradictions' will be revealed, equilibrium will be disturbed, and if a new equilibrium is again established, it will be on a new basis, *i.e.,* with a new combination of forces, etc. It follows that the 'conflict,' the 'contradiction,' *i.e.,* the antagonism of forces acting in various directions, determines the motion of the system . . . in the first place, the condition of equilibrium; in the second place, a disturbance of this equilibrium; in the third place, the reestablishment of equilibrium on a *new* basis. . . . Hegel observed this characteristic of motion and expressed it in the following manner: he called the original condition of equilibrium the *thesis,* the disturbance of equilibrium the *antithesis,* the reestablishment of equilibrium on a new basis the *synthesis* (the unifying proposition reconciling the contradictions).[60]

One need only compare this formulation of the triad to Trotsky's formulation in the notebooks to see how Bukharin and Trotsky have translated the language of dialectics and dialectical laws into their own idioms and architectonic preferences.[61] In the second notebook Trotsky translated the triad into his preferred catastrophic architectonic in the following fashion:

> *The triad—is the mechanism of the transformation of quantity into quality.*
> Historically humanity forms its "conceptions"—the basic elements of its thinking—on the foundation of experience, which is always incomplete, partial, onesided. It includes in "the concept"

those features of a living, forever changing process, which are important and significant for it at a given moment. Its future experience at first is enriched (quantitatively) and then *outgrows* the closed concept, that is, in practice negates it, by virtue of this necessitating a theoretical negation. But the negation does not signify a turning back to tabula rasa. Reason always possesses: a) the concept and b) the recognition of its unsoundness. This recognition is tantamount to the necessity to construct *a new concept,* and then it is inevitably revealed that the negation was not absolute, that it affected only certain features of the first concept. The new concept therefore has by necessity a *synthetic* character: into it enter those elements of the initial concept, which were able to withstand the trial by experience + those new elements of experience, which led to the negation of the initial concept.

Thus, in the domain of thinking (cognition) as well, the quantitative changes lead to qualitative ones, and then these transformations haven't a [steady] evolutionary character but are accompanied by *breaks in gradualness,* that is, by small or large intellectual catastrophes. In sum, this also means that the development of cognition has a *dialectical character.*[62]

It bears repeating that Bukharin and Trotsky emphasize, respectively, a systemic architectonic, organized around the idea of the state of equilibrium of a system, and a catastrophic one, focused upon the moment of transition and discontinuous change in a process, without ignoring other architectonics. Thus, in Trotsky's essay on Kautsky quoted above he recognized "long ages of relative equilibrium," just as Bukharin recognized and affirmed catastrophes in systemic processes in *Historical Materialism,* for example. A little reflection reveals that the catastrophic architectonic in dialectics must nest, so to speak, within an epigenetic one, and the latter within the systemic architectonic, for breaks can only occur when a process of development has been identified, and what is developing is a systemic whole. Each thinker's translation of the Hegelian notion of the triad reflects an emphasis within dialectics, not a repudiation of the other principles.

Lenin provides us with still a third example of emphases within the architectonic complex subsumed under the term "dialectics." His *Philosophical Notebooks* provide an excellent illustra-

Dialectics and Evolutionism 61

tion, for they clearly promote the dialectical law of the interpenetration of opposites. The section of the notebooks entitled "A Conspectus of Hegel's Book 'The Science of Logic' " is especially germane. Like Trotsky's notebooks, Lenin's notebooks on Hegel and dialectics were not published during his lifetime and, unlike *Materialism and Empirio-Criticism,* did not have an immediate target. They too have an air of open-minded inquiry about them, a spirit of discovery. In a sense, Lenin confirms Eastman's statement of 1927, written before the publication of the notebooks, to the effect that dialectics meant for Lenin "*flexibility*—a maximum of flexibility as opposed to the 'pedantry' of ordinary intellectualism." In this vein Lenin wrote: "All-sided, universal flexibility of concepts, a flexibility reaching to the identity of opposites—that is the essence of the matter. This flexibility, applied subjectively = eclecticism and sophistry. Flexibility applied *objectively,* i.e., reflecting the all-sidedness of the material process and its unity, is dialectics, is the correct reflection of the eternal development of the world."[63]

For purposes of comparison with Trotsky, the heart of the matter is contained in a section where Lenin details the "elements" of dialectics. There are sixteen of them. In the first three Lenin takes his stand on objective materialism, holism, and development. He expresses fidelity to the systemic and epigenetic architectonics. However, it is clear that he is most impressed with the way in which contradiction emerges, in which opposites perpetually appear and struggle with one another, without destroying the integrity of the unfolding process in its totality. When Lenin discusses transition, he too recognizes that dialectical transitions imply an interruption of gradualness, a leap, but in his enumeration of the elements of dialectics he connects the catastrophic principle to the idea of the transformation of things into their opposites. These are the relevant passages:

> (4) the internally contradictory *tendencies* (and aspects) in this thing.
> (5) the thing (phenomenon, etc.) as the sum *and unity of opposites.*

(6) *the struggle,* or unfolding, of these opposites, contradictory strivings, etc.

(7) the union of analysis and synthesis—the breakdown of the separate parts and the totality, the summation of these parts.

(8) the relations of each thing (phenomenon, etc.) are not only manifold, but general, universal. Each thing (phenomenon, process, etc.) is connected with *every other.*

(9) not only the unity of opposites but the *transitions of every* determination, quality, feature, aspect, property, into *every* other [into its opposite?]. . . .

(15) the struggle of content with form and conversely. The throwing off of the form, the transformation of the content.

(16) the transition of quantity into quality and *vice versa.* (15 and 16 are *examples* of 9.)

In brief, dialectics can be defined as the doctrine of the unity of opposites. This embodies the essence of dialectics, but it requires explanation and development.[64]

This, then, is Lenin's translation of Hegel's laws of dialectics into his own stylistic emphasis upon the dialectical architectonic proper. He clearly emphasizes opposition, conflict, and struggle within process: "The unity (coincidence, identity, equal action) of opposites is conditional, temporary, transitory, relative. The struggle of mutually exclusive opposites is absolute, just as development and motion are absolute."[65] Thus, the transition from quantity into quality, which Trotsky believed was the most important law of dialectics, in Lenin was subordinated to the law of the interpenetration of opposites, with special emphasis upon struggle rather than systemic unity or wholeness.

There is nothing subtle about the translations of dialectics into individual styles in the cases of Trotsky, Lenin, and Bukharin. The peculiar emphases in the dialectics of the latter two have long been noted by serious students of dialectics.[66] However, students of Trotsky have not had much basis for sound statements about his style as a dialectician. The writings on science, technology, and psychology of the period 1922–26 provide clues, and so do later writings, but the notebooks, much like a point needed to establish a curve with certainty, yield sufficient evidence to estab-

Dialectics and Evolutionism 63

lish both Trotsky's emphasis upon the "first" law of dialectics and the persistence of his vision. His last known essays on dialectics, one of them written at the end of 1939 and entitled "The ABC of Materialist Dialectics," the other an open letter to James Burnham dated January 7, 1940, only confirm the remarkable continuity of Trotsky's position within dialectics.[67]

The last essays show the same use of Darwinism, the same emphasis upon the law of the transformation of quantity into quality. They also incorporate some of the metaphors and analogies which Trotsky used in his theory of cognition in the notebooks and reveal that his interest in the unconscious processes of the mind was an enduring aspect of his dialectical vision, an essential link in his theory of human development:

> Consciousness grew out of the unconscious, psychology out of physiology, the organic world out of the inorganic, the solar system out of nebulae. On all the rungs of this ladder of development, the quantitative changes were transformed into qualitative. Our thought, including dialectical thought, is only one of the forms of the expression of changing matter. . . .
>
> Darwinism, which explained the evolution of species through quantitative transformations passing into qualitative, was the highest triumph of the dialectic in the whole field of organic matter. Another great triumph was the discovery of the table of atomic weights of chemical elements and further the transformation of one element into another.[68]

In the open letter to Burnham, Trotsky repeats the warnings to Eastman of the period 1929–33: "Anyone acquainted with the history of the struggles of tendencies within workers' parties knows that desertions to the camp of opportunism and even to the camp of bourgeois reaction began not infrequently with rejection of the dialectic."[69] Trotsky could indeed point with some satisfaction to Eastman's career since the beginning of their controversy and to that of Sidney Hook, another critic of dialectics, as confirmation. Eastman moved to the right even more dramatically during the 1950s.

As for substantive positions, Trotsky defended the idea of unconscious dialecticians. Here, he put himself in a rather awkward position: He decided to show that animals used both the syllogism and dialectics and, alas, to credit them with instinctive insight into the first law of dialectics, the transformation of quantity into quality:

> Thus a fox is aware that quadrupeds and birds are nutritious and tasty. On sighting a hare, a rabbit, or a hen, a fox concludes: this particular creature belongs to the tasty and nutritive type, and—chases after the prey. We have here a complete syllogism, although the fox, we may suppose, never read Aristotle. When the same fox, however, encounters the first animal which exceeds it in size, for example, a wolf, it quickly concludes that quantity passes into quality, and turns to flee. Clearly the legs of a fox are equipped with Hegelian tendencies, even if not fully conscious ones. All this demonstrates, in passing, that our methods of thought, both formal logic and the dialectic, are not arbitrary constructions of our reason but rather expressions of the actual inter-relationships in nature itself. In this sense, the universe throughout is permeated with "unconscious" dialectics.[70]

Trotsky here fails to achieve the level of thought found in the last section of the notebooks, where he reflected deeply about the relationship between the dialectic of consciousness and the dialectic of nature and stated: "Since cognition is not *identical* with the world (in spite of Hegel's idealistic postulation), dialectical cognition is not *identical* with the dialectic of nature. Consciousness is a quite original *part* of nature, possessing peculiarities and regularities that are completely absent in the remaining part of nature."[71]

Perhaps the heavy irony that he employed in polemics prevented him from developing his views more perspicuously. Whatever the reason, a certain deterioration occurs in Trotsky's presentation of his views between the notebooks of 1933–35 and the polemics of 1939–40, and a seeming confusion of processes of mind and natural processes. We have, in a sense, returned to the origins of the notebooks and the Freud-Eastman idea of the residual animism in modern philosophies. It is useful to turn to one of Freud's few comments on Hegel and Marx, made in the thirty-

Dialectics and Evolutionism

fifth of the new introductory lectures on psychoanalysis, written at roughly the time when Trotsky was jotting down the notebooks:

> There are assertions contained in Marx's theory which have struck me as strange; such as that the development of forms of society is a process of natural history, or that the changes in social stratification arise from one another in the manner of a dialectical process. I am far from sure that I understand these assertions aright; nor do they sound to me 'materialistic' but, rather, like a precipitate of the obscure Hegelian philosophy in whose school Marx graduated.[72]

It is possible that Freud wrote these lines with at least some debt to Eastman, for he had read Eastman's *Marx and Lenin: The Science of Revolution* and praised it.[73] In any case, Eastman had applied an idea already there in Freud and had added to Freud's stature in the course of the book, something which Freud evidently appreciated. The idea that animism often clings to dialectical visions still retains its power, just as does Trotsky's notion that those who steadfastly hold to the dialectical persuasion are more likely to stand firm as revolutionaries. We are dealing here with emotions and not just cognitive matters. Trotsky expressed his own emotional commitment eloquently in his "Testament":

> I shall die a proletarian revolutionist, a Marxist, a dialectical materialist, and consequently, an irreconcilable atheist. My faith in the communist future of mankind is not less ardent, indeed it is firmer today, than it was in the days of my youth. . . . This faith in man and his future gives me even now such power of resistance as cannot be given by any religion.[74]

With this as a kind of introduction to the emotional underpinnings of Trotsky's position, let us now turn to the idea of the unconscious in Trotsky's notebooks and other writings, and its relationship to his biography.

Trotsky's Career and the First Law of Dialectics

At the precise time in May 1935 when he wrote his last entry in the notebooks—the entry which ends with the term "the unconscious"—Trotsky was suffering from one of those recurring periods of malaise that afflicted him during times of stress and was reading Fritz Wittels' book on Freud. One might infer from this that he was seeking insight into an apparently psychosomatic problem.[75] Yet he never attempted to apply Freudian analysis, either to his own career or to those of other political figures. Trotsky admired Freud's genius, but was fully aware of the problems in the psychoanalytic movement—perhaps directly, through his years in Vienna before World War I, most certainly indirectly through sources such as Wittels' book, which surveyed the heterodoxy in the psychoanalytic movement. In the second notebook, Trotsky went so far as to say that psychoanalysis is "frequently inclined toward dualism, idealism, and mystification."[76] Whatever his skepticism about some aspects of psychoanalysis, his attitude toward the idea of the unconscious was not unfriendly, as is suggested by his notion of "unconscious dialectics." He tended to see the unconscious mind as an inferior, yet developmentally essential, product of the evolutionary process.

In 1923 in *Literature and Revolution* he had clearly revealed his heroically rationalistic attitude toward the unconscious mind. Consciousness would control it, just as it would control all aspects of human existence, and harness it to conscious purposes. He espoused not only eugenics but what we now call biofeedback techniques for self-regulation:

> Man at last will begin to harmonize himself in earnest. . . . He will try to master first the semiconscious and then the subconscious processes in his own organism, such as breathing, the circulation of the blood, digestion, reproduction, and, within necessary limits, he will try to subordinate them to the control of reason and will. . . . Finally, the nature of man himself is hidden in the deepest and darkest corner of the unconscious, of the elemental, of the subsoil. Is it not self-evident that the greatest efforts of investigative thought and of creative initiative will be in that direction? . . .
>
> Man will make it his purpose to master his own feelings, to raise his instincts to the heights of consciousness, to make them transparent, to extend the wires of his will into hidden recesses, and thereby to raise himself to a new plane, to create a higher social biologic type, or if you please, a superman.[77]

Dialectics and Evolutionism 67

Roughly a decade after he had written these words, while still in exile on Prinkipo, Trotsky was permitted to travel to Copenhagen to address a Danish student organization. He gave a single lecture on November 27, 1932, during his brief stay there. In it he presented an overview of the Russian Revolution and ended with his vision of the future—a vision differing in no essential respect from that presented in *Literature and Revolution,* but he restated in slightly different terms his idea of what lay ahead:

> Anthropology, biology, physiology have accumulated sufficient data to place before humanity in its full magnitude the task of its own physical and spiritual perfection and growth. Psychoanalysis, no matter how one relates to one or another of its conclusions, has undoubtedly through Freud's genius put a lid over [given access to] the well called the psyche or, poetically, "the soul" of man. And what was found? Our conscious thought comprises only a fraction of the dark psychic forces at work in man himself. Research divers descend into the depths of the ocean and photograph the most obscure fish. Man's thought, having descended into the depths of his own spiritual well, must illuminate the most hidden motive forces of the psyche and subject them to reason and will. Once having gotten control over the anarchic forces of its own society, humanity will get at itself in the chemist's mortar and retort. For the first time humanity will see itself as raw material or, at the very best, as a physical and psychic half-finished product.[78]

Trotsky's idea of the unconscious mind in the passages quoted above is quite in keeping with the traditional dichotomy of consciousness and spontaneity in the social thought of Russian Marxists, and he took a fully Bolshevik position with respect to intrapsychic forces, a position which would not have troubled Freud: Consciousness, even if only a fraction of all psychic forces, must control the other ones. However, Trotsky's uses of "unconscious" usually suggest the notion of a lower level of development, and one not easily accessible, rather than a source of neurotic symptoms, as was the case with Freud; and, as shall be seen, Trotsky assigned the unconscious a positive role.

To return to the notebooks, Trotsky, distantly echoing his defense of Freud in the mid-twenties, gives consciousness relative autonomy from physiological forces and uses psychoanalysis in defense of the idea of the autonomy of psychological phenomena, but adds his own dialectical explanation:

> [I]t is precisely dialectical materialism that prompts us to the idea that the psyche could not even be formed unless it played an autonomous, that is, within certain limits, an independent, role in the life of the individual and the species. . . . All the same, we approach here some sort of critical point, some break in the gradualness, a transition from quantity into quality: the psyche, arising from matter, is "freed" from the determinism of matter, so that it can independently—by its own laws— influence matter. . . .
>
> When we make the transition from the anatomy and physiology of the brain to intellectual activity, the interrelationship of "base" and "superstructure" is incomparably more puzzling.
>
> The dualists divide the world into independent substances: matter and consciousness. If this is so, then what do we do with the unconscious?[79]

It is possible, with the help of his autobiography, to make several connections between Trotsky's notion of the unconscious and his dialectical theory. From the writings quoted earlier, it appears that he consistently tried to integrate an idea of the unconscious into a point of view embracing both nature and society, both Darwin and Marx. His ambitions had heroic Nietzschean dimensions, but they were quite rationalistic. He confronted the unconscious depths plumbed by Freud, even as he visualized dialectically mankind's climb toward higher and higher levels of development, with qualitative leaps interrupting the gradual ascent. Furthermore, he tended to see parallels between the process in its collective, social form and the intrapsychic process of individual creativity. Here too a leap took place after an accumulation of data, after painstaking labor, even if a scientist was unconscious of the laws of dialectics. Mendeleev and Darwin thus not only unconsciously gave examples of the law of the transition from quantity into quality in their theories, they *themselves* exhibited the same law in their creativity. When Trotsky described his own political creativity, his role as a leader, he also showed awareness of the role

Dialectics and Evolutionism 69

of the unconscious. It is time to turn to Trotsky's sense of his own creativity, as it is revealed in his autobiography of 1929, *My Life*.

Trotsky's relationship to the revolutionary masses in 1917 was undoubtedly the high point of his career. To be sure, his feats as organizer of the Red Army might be seen as an even higher point on a curve describing his career as a revolutionary leader, but the lyricism of his description of his meeting with the masses in Petrograd in the *Cirque Moderne* tends to support the view that his oratory in 1917 was his moment of supreme creativity in his own eyes. Once again, we encounter the idea of the unconscious, but now in a new light:

> I usually spoke in the Circus in the evening, sometimes quite late at night. My audience was composed of workers, soldiers, hard-working mothers, street urchins—the oppressed underdogs of the capital. Every square inch was filled, every human body was compressed to its limit. Young boys sat on their fathers' shoulders; infants were at their mothers' breasts. No one smoked. The balconies threatened to fall under the excessive weight of human bodies. I made my way to the platform through a narrow trench of bodies, sometimes borne on peoples' hands. The air, tense with breathing, exploded with shouts, with the peculiar passionate cries of the *Cirque Moderne*. Around and above me were densely compressed elbows, chests, heads. I spoke as if out of a warm cavern of human bodies. Whenever I made a sweeping gesture, I always brushed someone, and a grateful movement in response would let me understand that I should not worry, should not break off, but should continue. No kind of fatigue could resist the electric tension of this passionate human throng. At times it seemed as though you felt with your lips the insistent searching of this crowd that had fused into a whole. It wanted to know, to understand, to finds its way. Then all the arguments and words outlined beforehand gave way, receded before the imperative pressure of sympathy, and from a secret place there came forth fully prepared other words, other arguments, unexpected by the orator but needed by the mass. And then it seemed as if you were listening to the orator yourself, just a little bit off to one side, trailing behind his thought and being anxious about only one thing, that he, like a somnambulist, might lurch from the edge of the roof from the sound of your reasoning.[80]

Trotsky was quite conscious that he was using sensual images in his description of the relationship between the orator and the crowd. In a manuscript of the autobiography preserved among Trotsky's papers, he had crossed out the words "you physically felt in your entire body" and replaced it with "on your lips the physical pressure," only in the end to use the phrase "you felt with your lips the insistent searching."[81] The Russian phrase "iz podspuda," in my translation "from a secret place," has an archaic quality. Trotsky strongly wanted to make the point that side by side with conscious rational activity other processes that involved the entire self, including its primal, hidden, and ordinarily inaccessible resources, came into play at certain supreme moments in his life.

The point is made even more clearly in another chapter of *My Life,* where Trotsky makes explicit the comparison between the coming together of the conscious leaders with the unconscious masses and that of the creative breakthrough in the individual. Here, however, he is careful to point out that he is using "unconscious" in a "historico-philosophical" sense rather than a psychological one:

> Marxism considers itself to be the conscious expression of an unconscious historical process . . . a process that coincides with its conscious expression only at its very highest points, when the masses with elemental force smash down the doors of social routine and give victorious expression to the deepest needs of historical development. The highest theoretical consciousness of an epoch at such moments merges with the immediate action of the lowest oppressed masses who are the farthest away from theory. The creative union of consciousness with the unconscious is what we usually call inspiration. Revolution is the violent inspiration of history.
>
> Every real writer knows moments of creativity, when someone else, stronger than he, guides his hand. Every genuine orator knows minutes, when something stronger than he speaks through his lips. This is "inspiration." It issues from the greatest creative tension of all one's powers. The unconscious climbs up from its deep lair and subjects the conscious effort of thought to itself, merging with it in some kind of higher unity. The latent [podspud-

Dialectics and Evolutionism 71

nye] powers of the organism, its deepest instincts, its flair, inherited from animal ancestors, all of this rose up, smashed down the doors of psychic routine and—together with the highest historico-philosophical generalizations—stood in the service of the revolution. Both of these processes, individual and mass, were based on the combination of consciousness with the unconscious, of instinct, the mainspring of will, with the highest forms of generalizing thought.[82]

These extraordinary paragraphs at once bring together all the strands of Trotsky's thinking about evolution, history, dialectics, the unconscious mind, and his own creativity. The second notebook, written approximately five years later, confirms that Trotsky associated his own moments of supreme creativity with a breaking down of inner barriers, a transgression of boundaries, that occurred only rarely. These creative moments of synthesis, of wholeness, signify a leap to a higher level of achievement, and in this case, in Trotsky's case, the inspiration of individual creativity combined with the "inspiration" of history.

At the moment of revolution Trotsky was a whole man, a man in contact with his most primitive latent powers, his instincts, his willpower, and simultaneously in contact with the violent inspiration of history—the unconscious masses. Thus, primal instincts supply the driving force for our highest historical achievement. Trotsky too found a place for the genetic architectonic in his vision. At our most creative, when we have achieved wholeness—a union of our conscious and unconscious minds—we are like sleepwalkers. He used the image twice more with slight modifications in the manuscript of *My Life* but crossed it out, no doubt because he realized that it had been used before.[83] These passages from *My Life* capture Trotsky's most positive sense of self. He achieved his creative peaks during moments of transition, of transgression, of discontinuous change. He never functioned at his best, never fully realized his creativity, when confined within the boundaries of routine. The first law of dialectics, the catastrophic architectonic, therefore probably symbolized for Trotsky those supreme moments, those creative leaps and breakthroughs when he realized his charisma as an orator and his gifts as a writer. The idea of the unconscious became the nexus of his personal, historical, and dialectical vision, for in it resided the source of creative inspiration. Perhaps we might apply a similar analysis to Bukharin and Lenin, and find some experiential basis for their particular styles as dialecticians, their emphases within the architectonics of dialectics, but nothing of the sort will be attempted here.

We can only speculate where Trotsky's theory of the role of the unconscious might have taken him. He never seems to have pursued his interest in psychoanalysis and, as noted earlier, his last essays on dialectics were qualitatively inferior to the material in the notebooks and the brilliant passages in *My Life* just quoted. He tried to repeat Lenin's career and clung to the hope that like Lenin he would regenerate the revolution in a triumphal return. But had he channeled his energy elsewhere and decided upon a career as a writer, he might have amended Marxist theory to take into account the power of the unconscious in human affairs. And had he done this, he might eventually have come face to face with the vexing, psychoanalytically inspired questions raised by Eastman, particularly the question of animism. Trotsky had made the unconscious less a source of human misery—a realm of darkness and primitiveness—than a reservoir of primal energy. It is possible that his revolutionary vision includes a transposition to history of his own moments of creative breakthrough, psychological wholeness, and full vitality: the whole, creative individual writ large. Trotsky seemed to be aware of the dangers of such transpositions, for he had warned parenthetically in the second notebook: "Subjective dialectics must . . . be a distinctive part of objective dialectics—with its own special forms and regularities. (The danger lies in the transference—under the guise of 'objectivism'—of the birth pangs, the spasm of consciousness, to objective nature.)"[84]

In fact, Trotsky failed to heed his own warning and brought the unconscious mind into the birth process—the spasm of creativity. He had transformed the pessimistic Freudian vision of the role of the unconscious into an optimistic revolutionary one. The unconscious mind's resources might be pressed into the service of revolution. In this respect, Trotsky was a forerunner of thinkers like Marcuse, who not only saw connections between the repres-

Dialectics and Evolutionism 73

sion of Eros and social domination, but believed that the unconscious was not merely a burden, that it contained creative resources that might further historical progress. Thus, when read in the light of his other work, the notebooks show how Trotsky's translation of dialectics and his appreciation of the creative role of the unconscious yielded both self-affirmation and revolutionary optimism. Although Trotsky tried to explicate Lenin's genius in the notebooks, in the end they tell us even more about his own personality and vision.

3. The Notebooks in Translation: Hegel

Hegel
See the topic L. [Lenin]

Those who repudiate "dialectics" consider it to be simply superfluous, a useless playing with thought. Positive science is enough! Does positive science therefore exclude pure mathematics and *logic*?[1]

In fact, dialectics is related to logic (formal) as higher mathematics is to lower.

Hegel himself viewed dialectics precisely as logic, as the science of the forms of human cognition, but in Hegel these forms are the ones in which the world develops, in that in logical forms it is only [realizing] its material content. Dialectics is summarized by Hegel in a work called "Wissenschaft der Logik."

For Hegel dialectics is a logic of broader dimensions—in space and in time—universal logic, the objective logic of the universe.

The negation of the concept in itself.

If we visualize the fabric of life as a complex piece of knitting, then *the concept*[2] can be equated with the separate stitches. Every concept seems to be independent and complete (formal logic operates with them this way), in reality every stitch has two ends, which connect it with adjacent stitches. If pulled at the end it

The last page of the notebook on Hegel. It ends with the word "process" and a comma.

Notebook on Hegel

unravels—the dialectical *negation* of a concept, in its *limitedness,* in its sham independence.

Some objects (phenomena) are confined easily within boundaries according to logical classification, others present [us with] difficulties: they can be put here or there, but within a stricter relationship—nowhere. While provoking the indignation of systematizers, such transitional forms are exceptionally interesting to dialecticians, for they smash the limited boundaries of classification, revealing the real connections and consecutiveness of a living process.

According to Hegel *being* and *thinking* are identical (absolute idealism). Materialism does not adopt this *identity*—it premises being to thought.

"abstrakt, tot unbewegend" (I, 43)[3]
Sehr gut!

The identity of being and thinking according to H[egel] signifies the identity of objective and subjective logic, their ultimate congruence. Materialism accepts the correspondence of the subjective and objective, their unity, but not their identity, in other words, it does not liberate matter from its materiality, in order to keep only the logical framework of regularity, of which scientific thought (consciousness) is the expression.

"in ihrer Wahrheit das ist in ihrer Einheit"
I, 43[4]
Sehr gut!

The doctrine of the teacher is taken up only in ready-made results, which are transformed into a pillow for lazy thought. Hegel on Kant and his epigones. (I, 44)[5]

From Kant to Hegel (from dualism to monism)

Kant: Reason is self-legislating, it constructs its tools of cognition (the categories) by itself; only *the thing in itself* is located outside of consciousness.

Hegel: But the thing in itself is only a logical abstraction, created by reason; consequently nothing exists aside from Reason.

Is it possible to say that Hegel's *absolute idealism* is a *self-legislating solipsism*?

The concept—is not a closed circle, but a loop, one end of which moves into the past, the other—into the future.

If you pull at its end you can undo the loop, but you can also knot it. (This has been said once already!!)

Mikhailovskii[6] and others deduce the triad[7] from the *past, present,* and *future*. There is a shadow of truth here, but only a shadow. Our conceptualizing reflects *processes,* transforming them into *"objects."* Not every present is suitable for the formation of a concept; a certain *stabilization* of the process is necessary in order for an enduring representation of it to form. This act of consciousness is thereby a rupture with the past, which prepared the stabilization. Our concept of the earth, the "most durable" of our conceptions, the "most durable" of the objects of our everyday milieu, is based upon a total rupture with the revolutionary formation of the solar system. The concept is conservative. Its conservatism issues: a) from its utilitarian purpose, b) from the fact that the memory of a person, like that of humankind, is short.

Thus the triad does not at all correspond to an undifferentiated past, present, and future, but to the formative stages of the process,

The Notebooks in Translation:
The Second Notebook

1933–34

The session of the Council,[8] when Lenin is alone against four (1904). Martov[9] directs [the session]. He informs, gives reports, introduces proposals, his own amendments. Lenin is restrained. He isn't good at superficial repartee. Maybe at this moment I had flashes of doubt about my own powers. Uncertain notes were audible in his performances.

[(It is remarkable that Lenin nowhere mentions even a word about his brother, not even in passing—but the temptation must have arisen on more than one occasion.)][10]

Prison photos—two snapshots in a row, full face and profile, with tautly clamped jaws, with smouldering eyes—forced portraits, taken of captives.[11]

The terrorists, anarchists in exile were (little) annoyed by the Marxists, [they] stubbornly studied, spoke in their peculiar language, appealed to their shared ideas and authorities. [Two illegible words] the free spirit saw in Marxism an attempt to destroy its sentimental diffuseness and its right not to study.

Alliluev's[12] apartment, in which Lenin and Zinoviev had hidden from 6 July [1917] until 11 July (until the departure for Sestroretsk).[13]

The photograph portrays the apartment of a foreman or a highly qualified worker, [there is] a velvet divan alongside a writing table with a figurine, a bookstand with a few books, on the wall a print of "Death" by Beklin[14]—the artist holds a brush, behind his back a skeleton plays on a violin with a single string. During the years of reaction Beklin was very much in fashion—in Paris (?) the agent provocateur Malinovsky[15] also bought photo reproductions of Beklin's paintings.

Krasnaia letopis' [Red Chronicle], 1924, no. 1, in the appendix— a diagram of the revolutionary party, beginning with Catherine.[16]
(See this!!)

What an amazing chain of efforts and sacrifices!

Lenin's slogans:
"Down with the 10 ministers-capitalists!"[17]

Zubatovshchina[18]

Monarchy + social reforms
borrowed from Bismarck and Napoleon III,
a presentiment of fascism,
but all of this in truly muscovite style

The years of reaction
1907–1910 (a revival in the worker and student milieux begins at the end of 1910). The character of the collapse of the Bolshevik party in these years was almost total, complete. Provide a picture [of it].

Lenin was extremely late retreating (stigmas, exes).[19] This aggravated the decline, gave it an especially sharp character—but the decline itself was inevitable.

Two agents provocateurs even got onto the board of the St. Petersburg union of metalworkers (1913), and one of them, Abrosimov,[20] in the position of secretary of the board.

The Second Notebook   81

[(Lenin's examinations in 1891 in the law program: the list of questions sounds like an ironic introduction to the entire subsequent activity of the mightiest subverter of inherited and acquired rights.)][21]

On Lenin's handwriting

Graphology is a dubious science. To make a direct connection between certain features of writing with certain character traits—is too mechanical an approach to the psychological functions of writing. But there are doubtlessly features in handwriting, even without the rules of graphology. Despite all its distinctiveness, Lenin's handwriting is *streamlined*: it is an economical, expedient, quick handwriting.

[(Zasulich[22]—the first Russian woman terrorist—calls herself "a sheep!" (See her letter.)]

Undoubtedly, [the period of] *Iskra* [Spark] and *Zaria* [Dawn] was the time when Lenin was with a most highly qualified group of exceptionally gifted people, educated citizens of the civilized world.[23] Notwithstanding all [illegible word] the crotchets (Plekhanov's), a warm atmosphere of elevated ideas surrounded this group of six people. Lenin did not have the fortune ever again in the future to work in such a milieu. He himself became greater, but his collaborators were of significantly lesser dimensions.

The Politburo of the Bolshevik party even in the most

Lenin's new staff: Bogdanov, Ol'minskii, Lunacharskii, Vorovskii represented a deterioration.[24]

"Nikolai Lenin"[25]
Where did it come from?
Perhaps "N." in honor of his wife (Nadezhda).[26]

The politics of three dimensions. The revolutionary of three dimensions—in two senses: consistency as a revolutionary (but

Blanqui, for example, was like this too) and the ability to grasp all three dimensions of the situation from the standpoint of revolutionary action.

Lenin—Kautsky—Bebel[27]

Until 1914 Lenin regarded Kautsky as an authority—in foreign affairs. In 1906 with the greatest pleasure he seized on Kautsky's answer to Plekhanov's questionnaire, which underlined the significance of "authority" in the workers' movement. At the same time, whenever the authorities collided with the interests of the Bolshevik faction Bebel proved to be "a little old fellow," looking for a compromise, and Kautsky [illegible word]. Self-confidence!

Snapshots

Lenin in 1915 [*Proletarskaia revoliutsiia*, 1925, no. 1 (36), p. 52]

The photograph is not stagy, like a portrait, but contingent, accidental. This is its weak side. But it is also sometimes the very source of its power. The features of the face acquire a definition that they did not have in reality. The total absence of a beard accentuates even more the sharpness of the features of the face. The face is not softened by irony, slyness, good nature. In its every feature there is intelligence and will power, self-confidence, and simultaneously tension in view of the enormity of the problems of 1915.

The war. The International had collapsed. He had to start all the work over again, from the beginning.

Lenin in 1921 (in the same issue) is much more relaxed, less tense, one senses from the figure that part of its vast work is already behind it.

The Moscow insurrection of 1905

Almost nothing is known about Lenin's relationship in practice to the insurrection. This is not accidental. It is impossible that the relationship did not exist. Lenin lived (?) in Petersburg. The connection with Moscow was very basic. Evidently Lenin did not want to have a regular connection; and he did such a good job at concealing it conspiratorially that it remains undisclosed, even to historians.

But all the same, why didn't other members of the CC [Central Committee of the Bolshevik party], who had worked with Lenin in Petersburg, have any memory of it? This aspect is the most mysterious one. But even here an explanation suggests itself. There might not have been a decision of the CC. If there had been a variety of positions in the CC, then Lenin could and must have managed without the CC, "pushing" the matter through persons especially close [to him] who explained to those in Moscow who had to know, that Il'ich gives his blessings to such and such methods—with the aim of conserving strength—which was fully in the spirit of Lenin.

Lepesha, Rapoposhka, Martushka[28]

Martov's delicate, fragile thought halted, powerless in the face of major events. The hopeless limitations of this very clever man never showed themselves more clearly than in his history of Russian social democracy, already written in 1918, where he completely misunderstood what had happened, and counterposed to the mighty forces of history the old a priori constructions of the Mensheviks which had long since been smashed to bits.

The inflexible, "doctrinaire," "scholastic" Lenin indefatigably learned from events, but the realist Martov created for himself a lofty refuge aloof from the action.

Martov's intellect, psychology [was] feminine. From this issued his letters—a magnificent stream—better than his articles, and his articles—are better than his books.

Lenin represented an equilibrium of physical and spiritual powers. Why then, in some periods did he seem so unbalanced, "a maniac" notorious not only to his enemies, but to opponents in his faction as well, and at given moments—even to those ideologically closest to him? Undoubtedly, because what is involved here is not an equilibrium of average, normal, and usual, but one of completely exceptional powers. His farsightedness, willpower, ideological endurance complemented each other, but each of these qualities swung around to [confront] his enemies and friends with unexpected aspects and monstrous results.

Lenin, at times, erred not only in minor but in major issues. But he corrected himself in good time and used the mistakes of his opponents. An accounting of his correct and incorrect decisions shows an enormous credit. A whole row of persons can, with every justification, point to their correctness and Lenin's errors in given, sometimes very important, issues. The group *Bor'ba* [The Struggle][29] was correct in its criticism of Lenin's first agrarian program (the "cutoffs"); Plekhanov was right in his criticism of Lenin's theory of the development of socialism "from the outside"; the author of these lines was correct in his general prognosis of the character of the Russian Revolution. But in the struggle of tendencies, groups, persons, by far no one was able to yield an account with a credit like Lenin's. In this lay the secret of his influence, his strength, and [word begun but not finished] not in a fraudulent infallibility, of the sort portrayed in the historiography of the epigones.

The years of reaction (1907–1911)
This decline had frequent moments of animation and flashes.

In political organizations only either the most wholeheartedly committed revolutionaries or the agents provocateurs remained. All those in between departed.

Genius
[Is it] an individual anthropological phenomenon or a social one?

[It is] a combination, the interaction of one with the other.

"Selection" and "exercise"—the application of Darwinian terms to the formation of genius.

The Second Notebook

Plekhanov and Lenin

Compare the celebration of the 25th anniversary of Plekhanov's revolutionary career with [that of] Lenin's 50th birthday.

In his speech Plekhanov thanked [everyone] for the laudatory messages, spoke about himself, cited Gogol, Goethe, and Wilhelm Liebknecht.[30]

Lenin arrived after the salutatory speeches—the organizers, knowing that it would be unbearable for him, did not insist on his presence—and in his speech said that they should abolish jubilee celebrations, so as not to imitate the bourgeoisie and not to get all puffed up (!)

Slavophilism—[is] messianism—[a form of] revenge for backwardness.

But in Russian messianism there was consciousness of peculiarity, distinctiveness, originality (Tiutchev)[31]

The unity of opposites, leaps

(See my old articles)

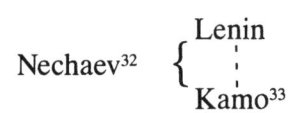

Nechaev[32] { Lenin
　　　　　　　Kamo[33]

The memoirs of revolutionaries, especially of those who did not play either primary or even secondary roles, are especially interesting. The lives of these people are constructed around one idea. Their horizon is often very narrow. The conditions of an underground existence tear them away from the world outside. Between arrests they resume some sort of narrow, sometimes purely technical task. Like a horse on a treadmill. They had every right to the bitterly ironic revolutionary nicknames they sometimes gave themselves. But at the same time, what a total concentration of spiritual powers, both on a single cause and a single external goal.

The Ulianov family[34]

Anna Il'inichna had no children (adopted ones?).

Vladimir Il'ich had none.

Mariia Il'inichna did not marry.

What about Dmitrii Il'ich?

Escape from Kiev prison and *Iskra*

The escape was possible given the background of the degeneration of the prison regime [thanks to] the students, and the sympathy of the bourgeois intelligentsia.

All the work of the old Iskra was like that

The historical backwardness of Tsarism armed it with a variety of resources unavoidable to Western absolutism. On the other hand, the historical backwardness of Tsarism armed the Russian intelligentsia with extreme ideas and . . . dynamite.

From this issued the passionate, tense character of the duel.

In the activity of *Narodnaia Volia* [The People's Will],[35] the element of surprise played a major role. The government was caught unawares. This was what yielded the effect. Later on it [the government] was prepared—and the effect disappeared.

Lenin's spiritual harmony—operated at such a high level—signified a gigantic expenditure of spiritual powers, and that upset [his] physiological harmony (See Professor Mel'nikov) [illegible word]

Lenin created the apparatus.
    The apparatus created Stalin.

$$a = a \text{ is only a particular case of the law}$$
$$a \neq a.$$

Dialectics is the logic of motion, development, evolution.

The Second Notebook

Formal logic involves stationary and unchanging quantities: a = a. Dialectics retorts: a ≠ a. Both are correct. A = a at every given moment. A ≠ a at two different moments. Everything flows, everything is changing.

What does logic express? The law of the external world or the law of consciousness? The question is posed dualistically, [and] therefore not correctly [for] the laws of logic express the laws (rules, methods) of consciousness in its active relationship to the external world. The relationship of consciousness to the external world is a relationship of the part (the particular, specialized) to the whole.

Logic involves unchanging qualities (a = a) and the fixed quantities of these qualities (25a). Dialectics is constructed on the transition of quantity into quality and the reverse.

The law of the transition of quantity into quality is (very likely) *the fundamental law of dialectics.*

In this sense dialectics is the logic of Darwinism (in opposition ... to Linnaeus[36] ...), the logic of Marxism (in opposition to rationalistic, idealistic theories of the historical process), the logic of philosophical materialism (in opposition to Kantianism, etc.)

The dialectical relationship to quality signified an entirely new relationship to so-called moral values. Official, that is, bourgeois thought today still views justice, rights, honor, as absolute values, as higher criteria. Dialectical materialism razed to the ground the kingdom of idealistic mythology. It showed how imperceptible quantitative molecular changes in economics prepare the way for a radical change in moral criteria: the old values are transformed into their opposite, against them new values enter the scene, the carrier of which is a new class or stratum, not seldom a new generation of the [old] class itself. It is quite usual in philistine circles to accuse Lenin of *cynicism,* and this expresses precisely hostility to the dialectical worldview, a struggle for absolute values, [both] essential for covering up [their] pitiful, barren, self-interested practice.

Alexander III [in] the 1880s was much more confident and decisive in the defense of autocracy than his father. "The great reforms"—especially the *zemstvo,* the judiciary, the press—made it possible for the bureaucracy to distinguish the true strength of its enemies and allies. The balance proved to be a favorable one.

Dialectics
It must be recognized that the fundamental law of dialectics is the conversion of quantity into quality, for it gives [us] the general formula of all evolutionary processes—of nature as well as of society.

Cognition begins with the differentiation of things, with their opposition to each other, with a classification of their qualitative differences. The quantitative definitions operate with independent particulars, consequently they depend upon qualitative definitions (five fingers, ten years, 100 amperes).

Practical thought lives within these limits. For a cattle trader a cow is a cow; he is interested only in the individual qualities of its udder. From his practical point of view he is indifferent to the genetic links between the cow and an amoeba.

If we grasp the universe from the point of view of atomic theory, then it appears to us like a gigantic laboratory for the transformation of quantity into quality and the reverse.

It is possible to acknowledge this, but to fail to make it the fundamental principle of one's own thought. There are those who unite the Kant-Laplace worldview with biblical faiths or quasi-faiths and, while advertising themselves as Darwinists, believe in the higher principles, the morals innate in humanity.

The principle of the transition of quantity into quality has universal significance, insofar as we view the entire universe—without any exception—as a product of formation and transformation and not as the fruit of conscious creation.

Hegel himself undoubtedly did not give the law of the transition

The Second Notebook

of quantity into quality the paramount importance which it fully deserves. Hegel relied upon the Kant-Laplace theory, but he did not yet know either Darwinism or Marxism. It is indeed sufficient to recall that the dialectician Hegel could consider the Prussian state the incarnation of the absolute idea.

Engels, following Hegel, called those who think in absolute and unchanging categories, that is, who visualize the world as an aggregate of unchanging qualities, metaphysicians.

In a more or less pure form "metaphysical" thinking exists perhaps only in savages. Among civilized people eclecticism holds sway. The laws of "evolution," of "progress," on the whole are recognized, but independent of them several absolute categories are accepted—in the area of economics (private property), in politics (democracy, patriotism), in morals (the categorical imperative).

Anglo-Saxon thinking is at the present moment the preserve of empiricism.

In the English scholar's head, just as on the shelves of his library, Darwin, the Bible, stand side by side, without disturbing each other. Anglo-Saxon thinking is constructed according to the system of the impermeable bulkhead.[37] From this issues the most stubborn opposition in the conservative Anglo-Saxon world to dialectical thinking, which destroys all impermeable bulkheads.

> *"The transition into its opposite"*
> Vernunft wird Unsinn[38]
> Wohltat—Plage

To view phenomena according to their resemblance or opposition means to see them according to their *quality*.

The transition of quality into quantity and the reverse presupposes the transition of one quality into another.

See Freud.

In primitive languages, big and small, high and low, etc., are expressed by *one word,* and the opposition between big and small is expressed by gestures, intonations, etc. In other words language, at a time when it was being developed, had only a general character, converting opposing qualities into quantitative differences.

The very same thing applies to the concepts of sweet and bitter, and at a later time—to good and evil, wealth and poverty, etc.

In these abstract formulas we have the most general laws (forms) of motion, change, the transformation of the stars of the heaven, of the earth, nature, and human society.

We have here the logical (dialectical) forms of the transformation of one regime into another. But in such general form it is a matter only of possibility.

The conversion of an abstract possibility into a concrete necessity[39]— also an important law of dialectics—is defined each time by a combination of definite material conditions? Thus, from the possibility of a bourgeois victory over the feudal classes until the victory itself there were various time lapses, and the victory frequently looked like a semivictory.

In order for a possibility to become a necessity there had to be a corresponding strengthening of some factors and the weakening of others, a definite interrelationship among these strengthenings and weakenings. In other words: it was necessary for several interconnected series of quantitative changes to prepare the way for a new constellation of forces.

The law of the conversion of possibility into necessity thus leads—in the last analysis—to the law of the conversion of quantity into quality.

Catastrophes

Everything flows, but not outside [its] banks. The world is not "fluid," there are changes in it, the crystallization of durable (con-

The Second Notebook

gealed) elements, although indeed not "eternal" ones. Then life creates its own banks for itself in order later to wash them away. The quantitative changes of matter at a given stage push against those congealed forms, which sufficed for its previous state. Conflict. Catastrophe. Either the old form conquers (only partially conquers), necessitating the self-adaptation of the conquered (partially) process, or the process of movement explodes the old form and creates a new one, by way of its new crystallizations from its wombs and the assimilation of elements of the old form.

See in addition

[John Stuart] Mill #

The liberal (gradualist) conception of development,

progress

The theory of revolutions

The logical antimony of *content* and *form* in this way loses its absolute character. Content and form change place. Content creates new forms from itself. In other words the correlation of content and form leads, in the last analysis, to the conversion of quantity into quality.

Continue in relation to the other antinomies.

What is the aim of this? says the contemporary "positivist": I can give an excellent analysis of the world of phenomena without these contrivances and pedantic subtleties. With equal justification a butcher will say that he can sell veal without resorting to the Aristotelian syllogism. To the butcher we would try to make clear that in reality he is always relying on the syllogism without knowing it; [that] if his trade is poor, then his personal ignorance cannot but affect it; but that, if he wants to set things up solidly, then he cannot avoid teaching his son the sciences, the composition of which includes the science of the syllogism (logic).

To the representative of positivism, with his limited point of view, we say that all the contemporary sciences [(at their head, those that involve matter, substance)] use the laws of dialectical thinking at every step, just as the shopkeeper uses the syllogism or as Monsieur Jourdain uses prose: without ever knowing it. Precisely because of this the average scholar preserves many habitual [traits resembling those] of impermeable bulkheads, not posing those questions which issue from the *general* movement of scientific thought, and cravenly ceases to draw general conclusions, when they call for a dialectical leap.

The dialectic does not liberate the investigator from painstaking study of the facts, quite the contrary: it requires it. But in return it gives investigative thought elasticity, helps it cope with ossified prejudices, arms it with invaluable analogies, and educates it in a spirit of daring, grounded in circumspection.

Etonnante découverte d'un savant italien

> Rome, 5 juin.—Une découverte exceptionnellement importante vient d'être faite par l'academicien d'Italie, M. Enrico Fermi.
> Celui-ci est arrivé à créer artificiellement un nouveau corps simple s'ajoutant à la liste des 92 corps simples existants. Ses travaux font suite à ceux des savants français Joliot et Mme Curie. Ceux-ci, après leur découverte du neutron, étaient parvenus à se servir de ce corpuscule pour "bombarder" le noyau atomique d'un certain nombre de corps simples; le corps simple ainsi bombardé se transformait en un autre corps simple, mais toujours dans la série des corps existants, c'est-à-dire de 1 (hydrogène) a 92 (uranium).
> M. Enrico Fermi, par le même procédé, a réussi à bombarder le dernier corps de la série, c'est-à-dire l'atome d'uranium.
> L'éclatement du noyau atomique bombardé a donné naissance à un nouveau corps appelé "élément 93."
> L'annonce de cette découverte a été faite, au cours de la séance de clôture de l'année académique, par le sénateur Mario Orso Corbino.[40]

The example of Mendeleev,[41] whose lack of dialectical method prevented him from recognizing the mutual transformability of the elements, despite the fact that his discovery of the periodic table of elements connected the quantitative differences among them to the quantitative differences of atomic weights.

Antinomies: *cause* and *effect*
  (cause and goal) in another order
  base and *superstructure*
  "*the interaction*":

that which is conceived $\begin{cases} \text{metaphysically} \\ \text{and} \\ \text{dialectically} \end{cases}$

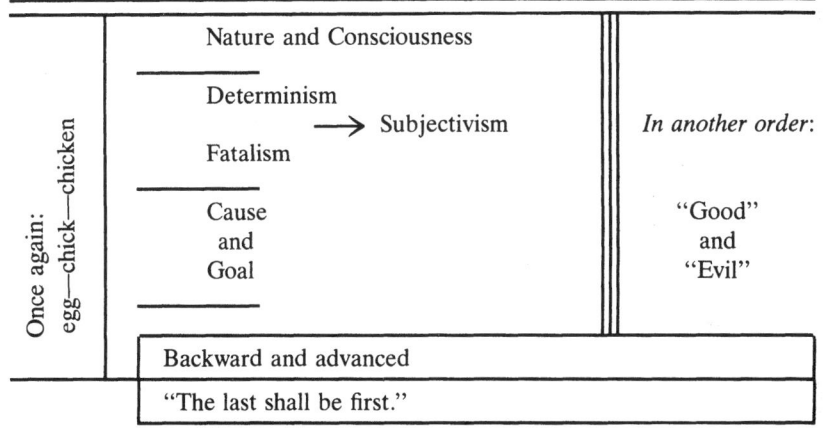

Once again: egg—chick—chicken	Nature and Consciousness	In another order:
	Determinism → Subjectivism Fatalism	
	Cause and Goal	"Good" and "Evil"
Backward and advanced		
"The last shall be first."		

Abstractness and Concreteness
"The truth is always concrete."

The Triad
Thesis—Antithesis—Synthesis
The negation of the negation

Judgment and Reason

National socialism

Elements of the dialectic penetrate all thinking in one or another degree, and even more so the thinking of "civilized" contemporary people who have experienced the greatest technological transformations, economic upheavals, wars, and revolutions. In the area of ideology, national socialism represents an extreme reaction against the dialectic, more weighty in its consistency than Italian fascism, which is eclectic through and through. Philosophical national socialism is aimed precisely against the idea of development: it therefore maliciously rejects not only Marxism but Darwinism—it wants to return cognition to static principles; with respect to human society such categories turn out to be *race* and *blood*. The power of dialectical thought here proves its strength by the method of reversal; consistent opposition to the dialectic throws one back to the depths of the Teutoburg Forest.

Lenin and Martov

If all contemporary thought is penetrated by elements of the dialectic, then this is even truer of the political thinking of the Mensheviks, who had passed through the school of Marxism and revolutionary events. But dialectics differ. Martov very subtly, in many cases, with great virtuosity commanded the dialectic. But this was a dialectic close to his thinking about phenomena in the intelligentsia milieu connected with the intelligentsia of the top stratum of workers.

Martov sometimes very intelligently analyzed regroupings in the sphere of parliamentary politics, changes in the tendencies of the press, the maneuvers of ruling circles—insofar as all this was limited to ongoing politics, the preparatory stage for distant events or the peaceful conditions when only the leaders, deputies, journalists, and ministers of prewar Europe acted in the political arena, when the basic antagonists remained virtually unchanging.

Within these boundaries Martov swam about like a fish in water. His dialectic was a dialectic of derivative processes and limited scale, episodic changes. Beyond these boundaries he did not venture.

On the contrary, Lenin's dialectic had a massive character. His thought—his opponents often accused him of this—"simplified" reality, indeed swept aside the secondary and episodic in order to deal with the basic. Thus, Engels "simplified" reality when he defined the state as armed detachments of people with material appendages in the form of jails. But this was a *saving* simplification: true, insufficient in itself for an evaluation of the conjunctures of the day, it was decisive in the last historical analysis.

Lenin's thought operated with living classes as the basic factors of society and thus revealed *all* its power in those periods when the great masses entered the scene, that is, in periods of profound upheavals, wars, and revolutions. The Leninist dialectic was a dialectic for the large scale.

Although the fundamental laws of mechanics hold for all man's productive activity, in reality there is the mechanics of the watchmaker and the mechanics of Dnepostroi.[42] Martov's thought was the thought of a watchmaker in politics. Lenin's thought worked on the scale of Dnepostroi. Is this a difference of a quantitative order? Quantity here passes over into quality.

The comparison with the watchmaker, however, has very conditional meaning. A watch's mechanism will live its self-contained life (so long as it is not ruined), and the watch's hands can correctly show the hour, even though the watchmaker is ignorant of the law of the earth's motion around its axis. But the politics of a minor scale (internal groupings within parties, parliamentary games, etc.) maintains its relative independence while the (relatively) large factors, that is, classes, are unchanging. Martov's dialectic therefore yielded the more tragic misfirings in matters of a minor scale as well, the closer the approach of stormy class conflicts, of perturbations in the life of society. And since our entire epoch since the first years of the century became one of ever more grandiose historical perturbations, Martov's thought increasingly showed its weakness, turned dialectics simply into a screen for inner uncertainty, and fell under the influence of vulgar empiricists, like Dan.[43]

To the contrary, Lenin's thought analyzed all the secondary phenomena, all the elements of the superstructure more penetratingly, the more immediately they depended upon the class movements that were occurring. From stage to stage Lenin's thought became stronger, more courageous, and at the same time subtler and more flexible.

Martov's mistakes were always and invariably mistakes *to the right* of historical development, they grew in frequency and in scope and soon outgrew the area of tactics and moved into that of strategy, and by virtue of that rendered nil the tactical resourcefulness and wealth of his initiatives.

Lenin's political mistakes were always *to the left* of the line of development, thus the farther [along the line of development], the rarer they became, the smaller the angle of deviation, the sooner they were recognized and corrected; by virtue of which the relationship between strategy and tactics achieved a higher and more perfect correspondence.

Materialist dialectics
(beginning)

Dialectics is the logic of development. It examines the world—completely without exception—not as a result of creation, of a sudden beginning, the realization of a plan, but as a result of motion, of transformation. Everything that is *became* the way it is as a result of lawlike development.

In this, its fundamental and most general sense, the dialectical view of nature and humanity coincides with the so-called "evolutionary" view of nature, the view of the contemporary natural and social sciences, insofar as they genuinely deserve this designation. One needs only to note that the philosophical conception of the development of all existence, representing a courageous generalization issuing from the preceding development of science, emerged before Darwinism and Marxism and either indirectly or directly enriched them.

We further will see that "evolution" as a general formula for the origins of the world and society is more amorphous, less concrete, with less content, than the dialectical conception. Now it is quite enough for us that the dialectical (or evolutionary) point of view, consequently the suitable one, inevitably leads to materialism: the organic world emerged from the inorganic, consciousness is a capacity of living organisms depending upon organs that originated through evolution. In other words "the soul" of evolution (of dialectics) leads in the last analysis to matter. The evolutionary point of view carried to a logical conclusion leaves no room for either idealism or dualism, or for the other species of eclecticism.

Thus, "the materialist dialectic" (or "dialectical materialism") is not an arbitrary combination of two independent terms, but is a differentiated unity—a short formula for a whole and indivisible worldview, which rests exclusively on the entire development of scientific thought in all its branches, and which alone serves as a scientific support for human praxis.

The liberal conception of "progress"
Vestnik Evropy [Herald of Europe],[44] sixth year, second book, February 1871
\#
Russia's commercial problems
The development of international trade links—to speak with the words of J. S. Mill—"being the chief guarantee of peace on the globe, serves as the great, solid security for the constant progress in ideas, institutions, and qualities of the human species."

Transpose here what was said about Clemenceau,[45] his attitude toward evolutionism, etc.

Note, how an egg "progresses" into a chicken.

The old sophism about the bald man[46] is the dialectical revelation of the unsoundness (= inadequacy) of formal categories.

Contrary to a photograph, which is the element of formal logic, the [motion-picture] film is "dialectical" (badly expressed).

Cognizing thought begins with differentiation, with the instantaneous photograph, with the establishment of terms—conceptions, in which the separate moments of a process are placed but from which the process as a whole escapes. These terms-conceptions, created by cognizing thought, are then transformed into its fetters. Dialectics removes these fetters, revealing the relativity of motionless concepts, their transition into each other. (S. Logik, I, S. 26–27)[47]

"We can investigate reality without the dialectic."

In the same way that we can walk without [knowing] anatomy and digest food without [knowing] physiology.

Hegel's absolute idealism is directed against dualism—against the thing-in-itself (I, 28)[48] of dualism. Isn't the recognition of the reality of the external world, *outside* a cognizing consciousness and independent of it, a return to dualism? Not at all, for cognition is in no respect an independent principle for us, but a specialized part of the objective world (make precise).

The evolutionary point of view is not at all hostile to our reason (Engels). Therefore we must study evolutionary logic (dialectics). Eastman[49] scoffs at this.

Reason, which would be present at the most distant evolution of the earth, at the origin of the solar system and at the development in it of organic life, etc., and would be able to embrace these processes, would be, so to speak, dialectical reason immanent at birth. But our human reason is nature's youngest child. To human memory nature offered not so much a picture of change, as repeating cycles, "the wind returns to its circuits." Humanity itself is a consecutive succession of generations. Each generation starts the difficult work of cognition in a certain sense from the beginning. Within the boundaries of everyday praxis people are accustomed to dealing with unchanging objects. As a result of this innate, inherited, automatized [practice] there appears rational logic, which dismembers nature into autonomous and unchanging elements. The development of thought makes its way from vulgar logic to dialectics only on the basis of accumulated scientific experience, under the spur of historical (class) development.

Rationalism is an attempt to create a complete system on the basis of vulgar logic.

The chronology of evolutionism
The *Kant-Laplace* theory of the origins of the solar system[50]
The dialectic of Hegel (after the French Revolution)
The theory of [Charles] Lyell (the evolution of the earth)[51]
The theory of Darwin (the origin of species)
The theory of Marx

In this fashion the transition from thinking in static categories to thinking in [terms of] development traces its lineage to the epoch after the Great French Revolution, which was the last great, brilliant burst of courageous rationalism.

Kant earlier believed that *logic* had been perfected because, since the time of *Aristotle,* that is, over a period of two thousand years, it hadn't changed.

Hegel to the contrary saw in this the enormous backwardness of logic.

The essence of the matter is that the rules and methods of a narrowly practical, common, or vulgar [mode] of thinking crystalized—entirely on the basis of praxis—and the theoretical work connected to it—very early, already in ancient times, and within the boundaries of this common thinking change was neither demanded nor tolerated. But precisely the growth and development of cognition on the foundation of Aristotelian logic prepared the way for its explosion.

The triad is the "mechanism" of the transformation of quantity into quality.

Historically humanity forms its "conceptions"—the basic elements of its thinking—on the foundation of experience, which is always incomplete, partial, one-sided. It includes in "the concept"

From the second notebook, the page with the heading: *The triad is the "mechanism" of the conversion of quantity into quality.*

The Second Notebook

those features of a living, forever changing process, which are important and significant for it at a given moment. Its future experience at first is enriched (quantitatively) and then *outgrows* the closed concept, that is, in practice negates it, by virtue of this necessitating a theoretical negation. But the negation does not signify a turning back to tabula rasa. Reason already possesses: a) the concept and b) the recognition of its unsoundness. This recognition is tantamount to the necessity to construct *a new concept,* and then it is inevitably revealed that the negation was not absolute, that it affected only certain features of the first concept. The new concept therefore has by necessity a *synthetic* character: into it enter those elements of the initial concept, which were able to withstand the trial by experience + those new elements of experience, which led to the negation of the initial concept.

Thus, in the domain of thinking (cognition) as well, the quantitative changes lead to qualitative ones, and then these transformations haven't a [steady] evolutionary character but are accompanied by *breaks in gradualness,* that is, by small or large intellectual catastrophes. In sum, this also means that the development of cognition has a *dialectical character.*

The new "synthetic" concept in turn becomes the point of departure for a new trial, enrichment, verification, and for a new *negation.* This is the place of the triad in the development of human thought. *But what is its place in the development of nature?*

Here we approach the most important problem of dialectical philosophy.

The interrelationship between consciousness (cognition) and nature is an independent realm with its own regularities.

Consciousness splits nature into fixed categories and in this way enters into contradiction with reality. Dialectics overcomes this contradiction—gradually and piecemeal—bringing consciousness nearer to the world's reality. The dialectic of consciousness (cognition) is not thereby a *reflection* of the dialectic of nature, but is a *result* of the lively interaction between consciousness and nature and—in addition—a method of cognition, issuing from this interaction.

Since cognition is not *identical* with the world (in spite of Hegel's idealistic postulation), dialectical cognition is not *identical* with the dialectic of nature. Consciousness is a quite original *part* of nature, possessing peculiarities and regularities that are completely absent in the remaining part of nature. Subjective dialectics must by virtue of this be a distinctive part of objective dialectics—with its own special forms and regularities. (The danger lies in the transference—under the guise of "objectivism"—of the birth pangs, the spasm of consciousness, to objective nature.)

The dialectic of cognition brings consciousness closer to the "secrets" of nature, that is, it helps it master the dialectic of nature too. But what does the *dialectic* of nature consist of? Where is the boundary separating it from the dialectic of cognition (a vacillating dialectical "boundary")?

Consciousness acts like a camera: it tears from nature "moments" and the ties and transitions among them are lost; but the object of photography, the living person is not broken up into moments. Rather, motion-picture film gives us a crude "uninterruptedness" satisfactory for the retina of our eye and approaching the uninterruptedness of nature. True, cinematic uninterruptedness consists in fact of separate "moments" and short breaks between them. But both the former and latter are related to the technology of the cinema, which exploits the eye's imperfection.

Verify how this problem is treated by Lenin and Plekhanov.[52]

Hegel himself spoke more than once about necessary concreteness, issuing from the immanent motion of "moments"—of motion which represents the direct opposite of an analytic procedure (Verfahrens), that is, of an action external in relation to the object itself (Sache) and innate in the subject. (I, 60).[53]

The Second Notebook

22/VI/1934

The identity of *Being* (Sein) and *Nothingness* (Nichts), like the contradictoriness of the concept of the Beginning, in which Nichts and Sein are united, seems at first glance a subtle but fruitless play of ideas. In fact, this "game" brilliantly exposes the failure of static thinking, which at first splits the world into motionless elements, and then seeks truth by way of a limitless expansion [of the process].

The role of the émigrés

All of the information about the West, including [what came] through the legal press (right up to the liberal [press]), came through them.

Legal and illegal Marxism
1905

Legal writers of Tsarist Russia not only did not say everything, they didn't think things through. In essence, they didn't express fully and often did not think through the main point. Remaining within the boundaries of legality, they emasculated their thought. The illegal press seemed to them "simplistic," "fanatic," "rectilinear." But when the days of freedom began, it turned out that the undergrounders, the émigrés, swept the journalistic field. Only they knew how to write the language of revolution. But this is the least of it: precisely from among the émigrés came the most talented journalists. This was no accident: politics calls for spirit, consequently, courage, and these qualities express themselves in style.

The identity of opposites

Little Paul says "donne!" both when he wants to take, and when he wants to give.

Le troisième centenaire du "Discours de la Méthode"
Nous avons reçu la lettre suivante:
Monsieur le directeur,
Le *Temps* du 13 février et celui du 15 ont signalé plusieurs des manifestations qui auront lieu, en 1937, en l'honneur de Des-

cartes. Il intéressera peut-être vos lecteurs de savoir que, cette même année, les philosophes du monde entier, réunis au Palais des congrès de la future Exposition, commémoreront le troisième centenaire du *Discours de la Méthode*. Ainsi en a décidé le huitième congrès international de philosophie, réuni à Prague en 1934; le neuvième congrès aura lieu à Paris en 1937, et sera un "Congrès Descartes"; en liaison avec la commission Descartes, présidée par M. Paul Valéry, les organisateurs de ce congrès préparent un programme qui illustrera les aspects universels de la pensée de Descartes.

Veuillez agréer, monsieur le directeur, l'assurance de mes sentiments de haute considération.
Emile Bréhier,
professeur à la Sorbonne.[54]

Why on a given stage of development of scientific thought in various areas is it necessary to put a theory "on its legs" (the presumption being that it has been standing on its head until that moment?)

Because humankind in its practical activity is inclined to view the entire world as a means, and itself as the end. Practical egocentrism (homocentrism)—is carried over into theory—turns the entire world structure on its head. From this issues the need for corrections (Kant-Laplace, Lyell, Darwin, Marx).

The brain is the material substrate of consciousness. Does this mean that consciousness is simply a form of "manifestation" of the physiological processes in the brain? If this were the state of affairs, then one would have to ask: What is the need for consciousness? If consciousness has no *independent* function, which rises *above* physiological processes in the brain and nerves, then it is unnecessary, useless; it is harmful because it is a superfluous complication—and what a complication!

The presence of consciousness and its crowning by logical thought can be biologically and socially "justified" only in the event that it yields positive vital results beyond those which are achieved by the system of unconscious reflexes. This presupposes not only the autonomy of consciousness (within certain limits) from automatic

From the second notebook, some of Trotsky's reflections on the autonomy of consciousness.

processes in the brain and nerves, but the ability of consciousness to influence the action and functions of the body as well. What kind of switches serving consciousness are there for achieving these goals? These switches clearly cannot possess a material character, or else they would be included in the chain of anatomic-physiological processes of the organism and could not play an independent role consisting of their prescribed functions. Thought operates by its own laws, which we can call the laws of logic; with their help achieving certain practical outcomes, it switches on the last (with more or less success) in the chain of our life activities.

It is well known that there is an entire school of psychiatry ("psychoanalysis," Freud) which in practice completely removes itself from physiology, basing itself upon the inner determinism of psychic phenomena, such as they are. Some critics therefore accuse the school of Freud of idealism. That psychoanalysts are frequently inclined toward dualism, idealism, and mystification. Thus, Fr. Wittels (Freud, l'homme, la doctrine, l'école—French translation)[55] admonishes his teacher for not daring "dépouiller complètement l'âme de tout ce qui est organique" (207). Insofar as I know, this is a fact. But by itself the method of psychoanalysis, taking as its point of departure "the autonomy" of psychological phenomena, in no way contradicts materialism. Quite the contrary, it is precisely dialectical materialism that prompts us to the idea that the pysche could not even be formed unless it played an autonomous, that is, within certain limits, an independent role in the life of the individual and the species.

All the same, we approach here some sort of critical point, a break in the gradualness, a transition from quantity into quality: the psyche, arising from matter, is "freed" from the determinism of matter, so that it can independently—by its own laws—influence matter.

True, a dialectic of cause and effect, base and superstructure, is not news to us: politics grows out of economics in order for it in turn to influence the base by switches of a superstructural character. But here the interrelationships are real, for in both instances

The Second Notebook

the actions of living people are involved; in one instance they are grouped together for production, in the other—under the pressure of the demands of the very same production—they are grouped politically and act with the switches of politics upon their own production grouping.

When we make the transition from the anatomy and physiology of the brain to intellectual activity, the interrelationship of "base" and "superstructure" is incomparably more puzzling.

The dualists divide the world into independent substances: matter and consciousness. If this is so, then what do we do with the unconscious?

Additional Notes on Dialectics and Darwinism: Discussion and Translation

These notes are filed in folder T3749 with other materials which Trotsky had collected as support for his interpretation of dialectics. The folders T3748 and 3749 contain a variety of documents: excerpts from articles by N. Mikhailovskii and N. Kareev, of the Russian school of "subjective sociology"; others from the correspondence and collected essays of early Marxist thinkers, Engels, G. V. Plekhanov, and P. B. Aksel'rod, the latter a powerful inspiration to Trotsky during his first exile in Europe; and still others from Russian scientists and historians of science, namely, K. Timiriazev and F. Fetter, on Darwin and evolutionary theory. Trotsky had also collected a great deal of material on Lenin as a dialectician and had taken excerpts from articles by several writers, among them N. Bukharin, B. Nevskii, and I. Luppol. It is clear that they provided either inspiration for some of Trotsky's ideas or support for them. Aside from documents of this sort, he collected newspaper articles on a great variety of scientific subjects—for example, simian embryology, dark stars, the tobacco mosaic virus, the discovery of moldavium, and the production of two heavier isotopes of uranium. He underlined sections of the articles with blue and red pencil and sometimes wrote "NB" at

Additional Notes   109

places in the text. The newspaper articles are taken mainly from the science section of the *New York Times* and the *Feuilleton de Temps* and range from July 1933 to January 1938. The notes on dialectics written on separate sheets are not dated, and the presence in the same folder of newspaper clippings covering a span of between four and five years makes it difficult to assign them a year, much less a more precise dating. At best, we can assume that the notes belong to the same period as the newspaper clippings. The word "Dialektika" is written at the top of most of the notes, excerpts, and clippings, although on occasion Trotsky used the headings "Dialectical Materialism" or "Darwinism."

The kinship of these notes with those in the notebooks is quite clear. Trotsky evidently sought to clarify his thinking about Darwinian evolution. One of its most attractive features, its nonteleological approach to nature, permitted dialecticians to substitute for divine purpose a "logic of development" and to interpret dialectical development according to their own visions. In Trotsky's published writings and unpublished notebooks, as was pointed out above, he emphasized discontinuous changes, leaps—catastrophes—in the process of development. In these notes too he stressed the dialectical law of the transition from quantity into quality. A note entitled "Dialectical Materialism" is one of two typed passages and it states boldly, "All evolution is a transition from quantity into quality." From these additional notes it is possible to summarize Trotsky's approach to evolution. He evidently saw two major paths to the formation of species: the endogenous catastrophe through the accumulation of quantitative changes, yielding a new species in a qualitative leap; and the formation of species through attrition among transitional varieties which elevates the surviving ones to the status of species. Here one may surmise that he had in mind the exogenous catastrophes of the sort described in the article on Kautsky, in which ecological equilibrium is disturbed by a sudden change.

Finally, Trotsky in these notes shows considerable interest in the dialectical reversal, a phenomenon for which he found abundant illustrations in the history of thought. But thought follows historical conditions in dialectical materialism, and even religious thought embodied dialectical wisdom about historical social processes. In the second notebook he illustrated this in the diagram with the antinomies, where he wrote, "The last shall be first." One should add that Trotsky had experienced a great number of reversals in his own career. Here too we may hypothesize that his appreciation of the dialectical reversal had biographical, psychological background. The notes only add confirmation to the general impression, gathered from both his autobiographical and theoretical writings, that his style as a dialectician had strong connections to a life punctuated in every major period by breaks and changes of affiliation, creative leaps, and reversals of fortune. Trotsky understood very well that political history had its own "paleontology." He had consigned the Mensheviks to the rubbish heap of history and had heard the very words of derision that he had thrown at Martov in 1917 hurled at him in 1927. He clung to the hope that the dialectic of history would yield still another reversal of fortune that would permit him to triumph over Stalin.

Additional Notes

Dialectics

The syllogism is absolutely correct only when it is a tautology, that is, when it is fruitless.

The syllogism is "useful" when . . . it is incorrect, that is, when it admits into concepts "clearance."

The entire matter depends upon the permissible dimensions of "clearance." Here is where dialectics begins.

The fundamental "cell" of dialectical thinking is the syllogism. But it [too] undergoes transmutation, changes, like the basic cells in various tissues of an organism change.

"Philosophy" = a toolmaking guild in relation to all the remaining guilds of science.

A toolmaking guild is not a substitute for production as a whole. In order to use a tool one has to know a special area of production (metal work, lathe work). When an ignoramus, armed with the "materialistic dialectic" tries to solve complicated problems in special areas intuitively, he inevitably makes a fool of himself.

On the other hand, the "specialized" scholar can do without a toolmaking guild, that is, can use a tool of his own making, but his work will clearly suffer from it (Darwin, Mendeleev, and [others]).

"Our Revolution" 1906
from *Kliachko*[56]

Herzen[57] called Hegel's philosophy the algebra of revolution.

Dialectics is the logic of development. Logic (formal) is the dialectic of motionlessness. Logic is a particular case of the dialectic, when motion and change enter into the formula as "0."

Cicero believed that between unquestionable truth and unquestionable falsehood there is a broad middle region of truth which depends upon the subject, on the person who is doing the reasoning:

ista sunt ut disputantur
(a verbatim translation is
impossible) depends upon the
point of view

The "engineer" plays the very same universal role in the social constructions of M. Eastman and other Americans that Robinson Crusoe played in the constructions of bourgeois political economists.

People orient themselves toward ideas in two ways: treating them either as arbitrary, unreal shadows, standing outside the world of facts in their material conditionality, or as almighty "factors" which command reality. Both views are false. The idea is a fact in a chain of other facts.

"With Hegel the dialectic stands on its head. It has to be put on its feet in order to uncover the rational kernel under the mystical hull." These words of Marx from the introduction to the second edition of *Das Kapital* (1873) more than once inspired critical wits to refine them.

But in essence the very same operation—to turn something over from its head and stand it on its feet—has been repeated in every area of human thought.

God created man.
Man created God.
―――
The earth orbits around the sun.
The sun orbits around the earth.
―――

"To stand on its head. . ." Eastman scoffs at this. Nevertheless, science like art is full of such reversals.

1. Cosmology until Galileo established the interdependence between movements of the sun and earth. Galileo did not repudiate this dependence, but turned it on its head.

2. Pre-Darwinian biology established the expediency of the structure of species, the correspondence (suitability) of organs to the conditions of life. From this it wound up with a preconceived system. Darwin did not reject the "expediency," the correspon-

dence of organs, functions, environment, but turned the interdependence on its head. In this brilliant reversal lies the essence of Darwinism.

To support this, citations about Darwinism.

3. Mendeleev and his periodic <u>system</u> of elements. For him the indecomposable individualities entered certain mathematical relationships to each other. Subsequent developments in chemistry turned these mutual relationships on their head.

All evolution is a transition from quantity into quality. The very concept of gradual, slow development signifies the achievement of qualitative values with the help of quantitative change. This works decisively in all areas.

Darwin's natural selection, which leads to the creation of various plant and animal species, is nothing other than the accumulation of quantitative changes, yielding as a result new qualities, a new species.

Whoever denies the dialectical law of the transition from quantity into quality must deny the genetic unity of plants and animal species, the chemical elements, etc. He must, in the last analysis, turn back to the biblical act of creation.

Teleological thinking

Tolstoy did not want to accept that he lived on this earth without a preset aim, like a bird that has fallen from its nest.

"It is important to recognize that god is the master and to know what he wants of me; but what he himself is, and how he lives, I will never know, because I am not his equal. I am the worker, he is the master." (Tolstoy)

Teleology and Determinism

All schools of subjectivism in one or another fashion are based on the contradiction between objective cause and subjective purpose. Determinism is the philosophy of objective causality. Teleology is the philosophy of subjective purposes. The attempt to set up a hostile opposition between them or to combine them eclectically is itself a product of philosophical ignorance. The purpose is a partial aspect of the cause. Teleology is only a special department of determinism.

Darwinism

Everyone recognized the process of formation of *variations* by way of natural or artificial selection, but many categorically refused to recognize the very same process for the formation of *species*. As long as the transitional forms are there, the unity of a species seems stable. But should the transitional forms disappear, the varieties would become species.

—[Every process has its material or nonmaterial paleontology.]

Darwin's doctrine started as a theory of the origin of species and became a theory of the evolution of the organic world.

The zoological geography of Darwin and Wallace—thanks to evolutionary theory is separated by a gulf from the zoography of Linnaeus, etc. (the role of paleontology)
The intermediate links have died out.
The history of language—is the paleontology of thought.

Along what lines did the *objections against Darwinism* proceed? The Dutch botanist De Vries,[58] the author of the so-called theory of mutations, tried to establish a *basic* distinction between the special features of variations and those of species, by virtue of which they could not cross from one to the other. (But De Vries was an evolutionist all the same.)
Until Darwin the question about the origin of species was considered to be "the secret of secrets."

Wallace on Darwin:
"I don't have . . . that inexhaustible patience for gathering a multitude of the most diverse facts, that surprising capacity to draw conclusions from those precise and rich physiological observations, that cleverness in designing a plan of experimentation and that gracefulness in execution, finally—that inimitable style—clear and at the same time cogent and precise—in a word, all those qualities that make Darwin a fully accomplished person. . . ."[59]

Some notes on Darwinism. In Trotsky's brackets: [Every process has its material or nonmaterial paleontology.]

(apply to a characterization of Lenin—show the consistency of [his] qualities in various areas)

Dialectics

Wallace—not only a Darwinist, but a scientist who independently arrived at the theory of the evolutionary origin of species (among them, humanity), spent more than a little effort to adduce evidence that there was an impassable barrier between human beings and animals in the area of intellect and morality, in other words, evidence for the divine origin of the "soul."

Wallace makes the same leaps in relation to the transition from inorganic to organic matter and the appearance of consciousness.

Evolution does not permit bargains: You either have to admit it or reject it.

Every reaction is bound to repudiate transformism.
National-Socialism cannot be reconciled with Darwinism.

4. Russian Text of the Notebook on Hegel

ГЕГЕЛЬ

См. тему Л.[1]

Отрицатели диалектики считают ее просто излишней, праздной игрой мысли. Достаточно позитивной науки!

Исключает ли "позитивная наука" чистую математику и *логику*?

Между тем диалектика относится к логике (формальной), как высшая математика к низшей[.]

Сам Гегель рассматривал диалектику именно как логику, как науку о формах человеческого познания. Но в этих "формах" развивается у Гегеля мир, причем в логических формах он только находит своё[2] материальное содержание. Диалектика изложена Гегелем в труде, который называется "Wissenschaft der Logik"[.]

Для Гегеля диалектика есть логика более широких масштабов—в пространстве и во времени—логика вселенной, объективная логика мироздания[.]

---

1. "Л." написано красным карандашом.
2. В тексте: "своего".

Отрицание понятия в нем самом
Если взять ткань жизни, как сложное вязание, то *понятие* можно приравнять к отдельным петлям вязания. Каждое понятие кажется самостоятельным и законченным (так с ними и оперирует формальная логика), на самом деле каждая петля имеет два конца, которые связывают ее с соседними петлями. Если потянуть за конец, петля распустится,—диалектическое *отрицание* понятия в его *ограниченности*, в его мнимой самостоятельности[.]

При логической классификации некоторые предметы (явления) укладываются в рамки легко, другие представляют затруднения: их можно отнести и туда, и сюда, и [*в сущности*]³ при более строгом отношении—никуда. Вызывая возмущение систематиков, такие переходные формы представляют исключительный интерес для диалектиков, ибо разбивают ограниченные рамки классификации, вскрывая действительные связи и последовательности живого процесса[.]

У Гегеля *бытие* и *мышление* тождественны (абсолютный идеализм). Материализм не перенимает этой *тождественности*,—он предпосылает бытие мышлению.

"abstrakt, tot unbewegend" (I, 43)
Sehr gut!

Тождество бытия и мышления означает у Г[егеля] тождество объективной и субъективной логики, их конечное совпадение. Материализм принимает соответствие субъективного с объективным, их единство, но не их тождество, другими словами, он не освобождает материю от ее материальности, чтоб оставить от нее только логический каркас закономерности, выражением которого и является научная мысль (сознание)[.]

---

3. Здесь и далее в квадратные скобки, курсивом, взяты зачеркнутые Троцким в дневнике слова, но только в том случае, если они поддаются прочтению. Неразборчивые зачеркнутые слова опущены.

"in ihrer Wahrheit das ist in ihrer Einheit"
I, 43
Sehr gut!

Доктрина учителя берется только в готовых результатах, которые превращаются в подушку для ленивой мысли. Гегель о Канте и его эпигонах (I, 44)

От Канта к Гегелю (от дуализма к монизму)

Кант: Разум самозаконен, он сам строит свои орудия познания (категории); вне сознания находится только *вещь в себе*.

Гегель: Но вещь в себе есть лишь логическая абстракция, созданная разумом; следовательно, вне Разума нет ничего.

Можно ли сказать, что *абсолютный идеализм* Гегеля есть *самозаконный солипсизм*?

Понятие—не замкнутое кольцо, а петля, один конец которой идет в прошлое, другой—в будущее.

Потянув за конец, можно распустить петлю, но можно и затянуть ее в мертвый узел (Уже раз сказано!!)

Михайловский и другие сводят триаду из *прошлого, настоящего* и *будущего*. Тут есть тень правды, но только тень. Наши понятия отражают *процессы*, превращая их в "*предметы*". Не всякое настоящее пригодно для формирования понятия; нужна известная *стабилизация* процесса, чтоб позволить сформироваться устойчивому представлению о нем. [*Но*] Этот акт сознания есть тем самым разрыв с прошлым, которое подготовило стабилизацию. Наше понятие о земле, наиболее "устойчивое" из наших понятий о наиболее "устойчивом" из предметов нашего обихода, [*еще вмещает кое-как землетрясение, но со*] основано на полном разрыве с революционным формированием солнечной системы. Понятие консервативно. Его консерватизм вытекает:

а) из его утилитарного назначения, б) из того факта, что память человека, как и человечества, коротка.

Таким образом триада соответствует вовсе не безличному прошлому, настоящему и будущему, а формообразующим этапам процесса,[4]

---

4. Здесь обрываются записи в тетради Троцкого "Гегель".

5. Russian Text of the Second Notebook

1933–1934

Заседание *Совета,* когда Ленин один против четырех (1904). Руководит Мартов. Он информирует, докладывает, вносит предложения, поправки от себя. Ленин сдержан. Ему не хватает беглой находчивости. Возможно, что в этот момент у меня мелькали сомнения в собственный силах. В его выступлениях слышатся ноты неуверенности.

[*Замечательно, что Л*[*енин*] *нигде ни словом не упоминает о своем брате, хотя бы мимоходом—а искушение должно было возникнуть не раз.*]

Тюремные карточки—два снимка рядом, анфас и в профиль, с сурово сжатыми челюстями, с затаенными глазами,—подневольные портреты, снятые с пленников.

Террористов, анархистов (мало) в ссылке раздражали марксисты, упорно учившиеся, говорившие на своем особом языке, апеллировавшие к общим для них идеям и авторитатам,[**][1] вольница, [*не желавшая учиться,*] видела в марк-

---

1. Здесь и далее этим знаком обозначаются неразборчиво написанные, а потому опущеные слова рукописи. Количество * соответствует числу опущеных слов.

сизме покушение на ее сантимент[альную] расплывча-[то]сть и на ее право не учиться.

Квартира Аллилуева, на которой Ленин с Зиновьевым скрывались с 6 по 11 июля [1917 года] (до отьезда в Сестрорецк)

По фотографии квартира мастера или высококвалиф[ицированного] рабочего, бархатный диван у письм[енного] стола и статуэтка, этажерка с несколькими книгами, на стене гравюра "Смерть" Беклина—художник с кистью, за спиной его скелет наигрывает на скрипке с одной струной. За годы реакции Беклин очень вошел в моду,—провокатор Малиновский в Париже (?) тоже покупал снимки с картин[ами] Беклина.

"Кр[асная] Лет[опись]", 1924, № 1, в приложении—схема рев[олюционной] партии, начиная с Екатерины.
(СМ. !!)
Какая поразительная цепь усилий и жертв!

Лозунги Ленина:
"Долой 10 министров-капиталистов!"

Зубатовщина
Монархия + соц[иальные] реформы[,] заимствованные у Бисмарка и Напол[еона] III, предчувствие фашизма,
но все это в истинно московском стиле[.]

ГОДЫ РЕАКЦИИ

1907–1910 (в конце 1910 начинается оживление в раб[очей] среде и студенчестве). Распад б[ольшевист]ской партии в эти годы имел почти полный законченный характер. Дать картину.

Ленин сильно запоздал с отступлением (пятна, эксы). Это усилило распад, придало ему особую остроту,—но сам[2] распад был неизбежен.

2. В тексте: "самым".

2 провокатора входили даже в Правление петербургского союза металлистов (1913), причем один, Абросимов, в качестве секретаря Правления

[*Экзамены Ленина в 1891 г. по программе права: перечень вопросов звучит, как ироническая интродукция ко всей последующей деятельности этого величайшего ниспровергателя унаследованных и благоприобретенных прав.*]

О почерке Ленина
Графология есть сомнительная наука. Приводить определенные черт[ы] письма в постоянную связь с опред[еленными] чертами характера—слишком механический подход к психологической функции письма. Но есть черты в почерке, которые бесспорны и без правил графологии. Почерк Ленина при всем своем своеобразии *рационализован*: это экономный, целесообразный, скорый почерк.

[*Засулич—первая русская террористка—называет себя "овцой"! (См. ее письмо)*]
Несомненно, что "Искра" и "Заря" это время, когда Ленин был в наиболее высоко квалифицированной группе людей, исключит[ельно] даровит[ых], образованных граждан цивилизованного мира. Несмотря на все [*] капризы (Плеханов), над этой группой шестерых веял горячий воздух высоких идейных интересов. Никогда в дальнейшем Ленину не пришлось более работать в таком окружении. Сам он стал больше, но сотрудники его значительно меньше.

Политбюро б[ольшевист]ской партии даже в самые
Новый штаб Ленина:
Богданов, Ольминский, Луначарский, Воровский представляли снижение.

"Николай Ленин"
Откуда?
Может быть, Н. в честь жены (Надежды)

Политика трех измерений. Революционер трех измерений—в двух смыслах закономерность как революционера (но таким был, напр[имер], и Бланки) и способность охватывать все три измерения обстановки под углом рев[олюционного] действия.

Ленин—Каутский—Бебель

До 1914 г. Ленин относился к Каутскому, как к авторитету—в иностран[ных] делах. В 1906 г. он с величайшей радостью подхватил ответ Каутского на анкету Плеханова, подчеркнув значение "авторитета" в раб[очем] движении. В то же время, там, где авторитеты сталкивались с интересами б[ольшевист]ской фр[акции] Бебель оказывался "старикашкой", который хотел[3] мириться, а Каутский "[*]". Уверенность в себе!

Фотогр[афические] снимки

Ленин в 1915 г. ("Пр[олетарская] Рев[олюция]", 1925, № 1 (36), стр. 52)

Фотография не синтетична, как портрет, а эпизодична, случайна. В этом ее слабая сторона. Но в этом же иногда источник ее силы. Снимок 1915 г. в своем роде замечателен. Свет и тени легли резко. Черты лица получают ту определенность, какую не имели в натуре. Полное отсутствие бороды еще более придает лицу резкость чертами. Лицо не смягчено иронией, лукавством, добродушием. Во всех [*чертах*] лица ум и воля, уверенность в себе и в то же время напряжение пред неизмеримостью задач 1915 г. Война. Интернационал рухнул. Всю работу надо начинать сначала.

Ленин в 1921 г. (в том же номере) гораздо снисходительнее, менее напряжен, в фигуре чувствуется, что часть великих задач уже позади.

---

3. В тексте: "хочет".

Моск[овское] восстание 1905 г.
О⁴ практич[еском] отношении Ленина к восстанию почти ничего не известно. Это не случайно. Не может быть, чтоб этого отношения не было. Ленин жил (?) в Питере. Связь с Моской была очень проста. Очевидно, Ленин не хотел, чтоб эта связь была установлена. И он так хорошо законспирировал ее, что она остается невскрытой и для историка.

[*Возможно, что*]
Но почему же все-таки воспоминания не сохранились у других членов ЦК, работавших с Лениным в Питере? Это обстоятельство представляется наиболее таинственным. Но и здесь объяснение напрашивается [само] собою. Решения ЦК могло и не быть. Если в ЦК были разные настроения, то Ленин мог и должен был обойтись без ЦК, "подтолкнув" дело через особо близких лиц, которые дали в Москве понять кому следовало, что Ильич благославляет приемы—в целях экономии сил—что было⁵ вполне в духе Ленина.

Лепеша, Рапапошка, Мартушка

Ажурная хрупкая мысль Мартова останавливается в бессилии перед большими событиями. Ни в чем безнадежном органиченность этого умницы не выражается так ярко, как в том, что в своей Истор[ии] рус[ской] с[оциал-]д[емократии], написанной уже в 1918 г., он совершенно не понял того, что произошло, и могущественным силам истории противопоставив старую априорную конструкцию меньшевиков, давно разбился в дребезги.

Несгибаемый "доктринер", "схоласт" Ленин неутомимо учился у событий, а реалист Мартов [*доставав свою гибкую мысль не то чтоб*] создавал себе идеаль[ное] убежище в стороне от событий.

Ум Мартова, психология, женственна. Оттого его

---

4. В тексте: "Об".
5. В тексте вместо "что было": "были".

письма—поток великолепия—выше его статей, а его статьи—выше его книг.

Ленин представлял равновесие физических и душевных сил. [*В этом была его*] Почему же в некоторые [*его*] периоды он казался неуравновешенным, "маньяком", не только заведомым врагам, но и фракционным идейным противникам, а в известные моменты—и ближайшим единомышленникам? Несомненно потому, что дело идет о равновесии не средних нормальных и обычных, а совершенно исключительных сил. Его дальновидность, воля [*принципиальная*] идейная выдержка дополняли друг друга, но каждое из этих качеств поворачивалось к врагам и друзьям своими [*] сторонами и чудовищными выводами.

Ленин, случалось, ошибался не только в мелких, но и в больших вопросах. Но он своевременно поправлялся и использовал ошибки противника. Баланс верных решений и ошибочных сводился у него с огромным активом. Ряд лиц может с полным правом ссылаться на свою правоту против Ленина в определенных, иногда очень важных вопросах. Группа "Борьба" была права в критике первой аграрной программы Ленина ("отрезки"), Плеханов был прав в критике ленинской теории развития социализма "извне", автор этих строк был прав в [*вопросе о*] общем прогнозе характера русской революции. Но [*никогда но мо*] в борьбе тенденций, групп, лиц никто и в отдаленной мере не сводил своего баланса с таким активом, как Лен[ин]. В этом секрет его влияния, силы, а стало б[ыть] не в мнимой безошибочности, как изображает эпигонская историография.

Годы реакции (1907–1911)

В этом упадке были свои частые подъемы и просветы.

В полит[ических] организац[иях] оставались либо беззаветно-преданные революц[ионеры], либо провокаторы. Все среднее отошло.

Гений

Индивид[уальный] [*физиологический*] антропологич[еский][6] феномен или социальный?

Сочетание, взаимодействие того и другого.

"Отбор" и "упражнение"—применить термини дарвинизма к формированию гения.

[*Ленин*] Плеханов и Ленин

Ср. чествование 25-летия рев[олюционной] деятельности Плеханова и 50-летие Ленина.

Плеханов в своей речи благодарил за хвалебные приветствия, говорил о себе, цитировал Гоголя, Гете, Вильгельма Либкнехта.

Ленин пришел после приветственных речей,—устроители не настаивали на его присутствии, поняв, что ему это было невмоготу, а в своей речи говорил о том, чтоб отменить юбилеи, не подражать буржуазии и не зазнаваться (!)

Славянофильство—мессианизм—реванш за отсталость.

Но в русском мессианизме было и сознание особенности, отличия, своеобразия (Тютчев)

Соединение противоположностей, скачки

(См. мои старые статьи)

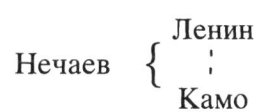

$$\frac{[P.S.\ 1934]}{[3]\quad [1897]}$$
$$[37]$$

Нечаев $\Bigg\{\begin{array}{c}\text{Ленин}\\ \vdots\\ \text{Камо}\end{array}$

---

6. В тексте: "антрополич[еский]".

Мемуары революционеров, особенно тех, что не сыграли ни первых, ни даже вторых ролей, представляют совсем особый интерес. Жизнь этих людей построена на одной идее [*которая очень украшена*]. Кругозор их часто узок. Условия нелегального существования отрывают их от внешнего мира. Между арестом и арестом они возобновляют какую-либо узкую, иногда чисто техническую работу. [*Они напоминают, когда*] Как лошадь на мельничием кругу. Недаром они сами себя именуют подчас с горькой иронией революционными клячами. И в то же время какая высокая концентрация всех душевных сил и на одном деле, на одной внешней цели.

Семья Ульяновых
У Анны И[льиничны] нет детей (приемные?)

У Вл[адимира] И[льича] не было

М[ария] И[льинична] не выходила замуж

У Д[митрия] Ильича?

Побег из киевск[ой] тюрьмы и "Искра"
Побег был возможен на фоне студенческого разложения тюремного режима, сочувствия бурж[уазной] интеллигенции.

Такова и вся работа старой "Искры"

Историческая запоздалость царизма вооружила его такими ресурсами, какие не имел западный абсолютизм. Историческая запоздалось царизма вооружила, с другой стороны, рус[скую] интеллигенцию крайними идеями и ... динамитом.

Отсюда страстный, напряженный характер поединка.

В деятельности Н[ародной] Воли большую роль играл элемент неожиданности. Пра[вительст]во было застигнуто врасплох. Отсюда—эффект. Дальше оно подготовилось,—и эффект исчез.

Ленинская духовная гармония—на столь высоком уровне—означала гигантское расходование душевных сил, а это нарушало физиологическую гармонию (См. проф. Мельников-[*])

Ленин создал аппарат
        Аппарат создал Сталина

a = a есть только частный случай закона
a ≠ a

Диалектика есть логика движения, развития, эволюции.
Логика формальная имеет дело с неподвижными неизменными величинами: a = a. Диалектика возражает: a ≠ a. Обе правы. A = a в каждый данный момент. A ≠ a в два разные момента. Все течет, все изменяется.

↓
Что выражает логика? Закон внешнего мира или закон [*мысли*] сознания? [*Закон*] Вопрос поставлен дуалистически, следовательно неправильно. Закону логики возражают законы (правила, приемы) сознания в его активном отношении к внешнему миру. Отношение сознания к внешнему миру есть отношение части (особой, специализ[ир]ованной) к целому.

↑ Логика имеет дело с неизменными качествами (a = a) и с определенными количествами этих качеств (25a). Диалектика построена на переходе количества в качество и наоборот[.]

Закон перехода количества в качество есть [*пожалуй*] *основной закон диалектики.*

В этом смысле диалектика есть логика дарвинизма (в противоположность . . . . Линнею . . .), логика марксизма (в противоположность рационалистическим, идеалистическ[им] теориям историч[еского] процесса), логика философского материализма (в противоположность кантианству и пр.)

Диалектическое отношение к качеству, означало совершенно новое отношение к так называемым моральным ценностям. [*Огромное большинство*] Официальная, т.е. буржуазная мысль рассматривает справедливость, право, честь как абсолютные ценности, как высшие критерии. Диалектический материализм не оставил камня на камне в царстве идеалистической мифологии. Он показал, как незаметные количественные молекулярные изменения в экономике подготовляют радикальное изменение нравственных критериев: старые ценности превращаются в свою противоположность, против них выступают новые ценности, носителем которых является новый класс или новый слой, нередко новое поколение того же класса. Столь обычные в филистерских кругах обвинения[.] [*То, что*] [Обвинения] Ленину в *цинизме* выражают именно вражду к диалектическому миросозерцанию, борьбу за абсолютные ценности, необходимые для прикрытия жалкой, скудной, корыстной практики.

Александр III [в] 80–[е] годы был гораздо увереннее и решительнее в защите самодержавия, чем его отец. [*Эпоха*] "Великие реформ[ы]"—особенно земство, суд, печать—дали бюрократии возможность определить действительные силы врагов и союзников. Баланс оказался благоприятным.[7]

ДИАЛЕКТИКА

Основным законом диалектики надо признать переход количества в качество, ибо он дает общую форму всего эволюционного процесса—природы, как и общества.

[Человеческое] Познание начинается с различения [*качеств*] вещей, с их противопоставления друг другу, с классификации их качественных отличий. Количественные определения [*получают*] оперируют с самостоятельными особями, следовательно опираются на качественные определения (5 пальцев, 10 лет, 100 [*овец*] амперов).

---

7. В дневнике Троцкого данный отрывок вставлен в предыдущий между словами "т.е." и "буржуазная мысль".

В этих рамках живет практическое мышление. Для торговца скотом [*овца*] корова есть корова; его интересуют лишь [*ее*] индивидуальные качества ее вымени. Генетическая связь коровы с амебой для него практически безразлична.

Если мы охватим [*вселенную,*] с точки зрения атомистической теории вселенную, то она предстанет перед нами, как гигантская лаборатория по превращению количества в качество и обратно.

Можно это признать на словах, но не сделать из [*его*] этого признания основной принцип собственного мышления. Есть люди, которые кантолаплассовскую теорию мироздания соединяют с библейскими верованиями или полуверования[ми], и объявляя себя дарвинистами, верят в вечные принципы морали, врожденные человеку.

Принцип перехода количества в качество имеет универсальное значение, поскольку мы рассматриваем всю вселенную—без всяких изъятий, как продукт образования и преобразова[ния], а не как плод сознательного творения.

Сам Гегель, несомненно, не отводил закон[у] перехода количества в качество того первенствующего места, на которые он имеет все права. Гегель опирался на теории Канта-Лапласса, но он не знал еще ни дарвинизма, ни марксизма. Достаточно в самом деле напомнить, что диалектик Гегель мог считать прусское гос[ударст]во воплощением абсолютной идеи[.]

Людей, которые мыслят в абсолютных и неизменных категориях, т.е. представляют себе мир, как совокупность [*переходящих*] неизменных качеств, Энгельс вслед за Гегелем называл метафизиками.

В более или менее чистом своем виде "метафизическое" мышление существует разве у дикарей. Среди цивилизованного человечества господствует эклектика. Законы "эволюции", "прогресса" признаются в общем и целом, но независимо от них признаются некоторые абсолютные категории,—в области экономики (част[ной] собств[енности]), политики (демокр[атия], патриотизм), морали (категорич[еский] императив).

Англо-саксонское мышление является и сейчас заповедником эмпиризма[.]
[*Дарвинизм Ученые английской*]
В голове ученого англичанина, как на полках его библиотеки[,] Дарвин, Библия, стоят рядом, [*как части целого,*] не мешая друг другу. [*Благодаря*] Англосаксонское мышление построено на системе [*коробочек*] непроницаемых переборок. Отсюда именно в консервативном англосаксонском мире наиболее упорное сопротивление диалектическому мышлению, которое разрушает все непроницаемые переборки.

"*Переход в свою противоположность*"
Vernunft wird Unsinn
Wohltat—Plage.

Рассматривать явления по их сходству или противоположности, значит рассматривать их по их *качеству*.

Переход качества в количество и обратно предполагает переход одного качества в другое качество.

См. у Фрейда.

в первобытных языках большой и малый, высокий и низкий и пр. выражается *одним словом*, и противоположность между большим и малым выражается жестом интонации и пр. Другими словами, язык в тот период, когда он вырабатывается, характеризует только общее качество, превращая противоположности качеств в количественные различия[.]

То же самое относится к понятиям сладкий и горький, а в дальнейшем—добрый и злой, богатый и бедный и пр[.]

В этих абстрактных формулах мы имеем самые общие законы (формы) движения, изменения, превращений звездной вселенной, земли, природы и человеческого общества.

Мы имеем здесь логические (диалектические) формы

превращения одного [*состояния*] режима в друг[ой]. Но в такой общей форме дело идет лишь о возможности[.]

Превращение абстрактной возможности в конкретную необходимость—тоже важный закон диалектики—определяется каждый раз сочетанием определенных материальных условий? Так, от возможности для буржуазии победить феод[альные] классы до самой победы проходили [*большие*] разные сроки, причем победа имела нередко характер полупобеды.

Чтоб возможность стала необходимостью, нужно было соответствен[ное] усил[ение] одних факторов, ослабление други[х], определенное взаимоотношение между этим усилением и этим ослаблением. Другими словами: нужно было,[8] чтобы несколько взаимно связанных рядов количественных изменений подготовили новую констеляцию сил.

Закон превращения возможности в необходимость сводится таким образом—в последнем счете—к закону превращения количества в качество[.]

Катастрофы

Все течет, но не вне берегов.

Мир не "жидок", в нем есть изменения и кристализация твердые (застывшие) элементы, хотя и не "вечные". Потом жизнь сам[а] создает себе свои берега [*и сама*], чтобы затем размыть их. Количественные изменения материи наталкиваются на известном этапе на те застывшие формы, которые отвечали предшествующему ее состоянию. Конфликт. Катастрофа. Побеждает либо старая форма (побеждает лишь частично), вынуждая побежденный (частично) процесс приспособиться, либо же процесс движения взрывает старую форму и творит новую, путем новой кри-

---

8. В тексте: "нужен был".

сталлизации из своих недр и ассимилизации элементов старой формы.

См. дальше
Милль

#

Либеральное (постепеновное) понимание развития, прогресса

Теория революции

Логическая антиномия *содержания* и *формы* теряет[,] таким образом, свой абсолютный характер. Содержание и форма меняются местами. Содержание творит из себя новую форму. Другими словами[,] соотношение между содержанием и формой сводится в последнем счете к превращению количества в качество[.]

Продолжить в отношении других антиномий[.]

К чему же это?[—]скажет современный "позитивист": я могу прекрасно анализировать мир явлений без этих ухищрений и педантских тонкостей. С таким же правом мясник скажет, что он может продавать телятину, не прибегая к силлогизму Аристотеля[.] Мяснику мы попытаемся разъяснить, что в действительности он [*пользуется*] [*опирается на силлогизм*] [*говорит*] на каждом шагу прибегает к силлогизму, не зная того; если его торговля мала, то его личное невежество может и не отразиться на ней; но что если он хочет поставить дело на широкую ногу, то не миновать ему обучать своего сына наукам, в состав которых входит и наука силлогизма (логика)[.]

Органиченному представителю позитивной науки мы скажем, что все современные науки [*в первую голову те, которые имеют дело с материей, с вещью*] пользуются на каждом шагу законами диалектического мышления, так же как лавочник пользуется силлогизмом, или как Журден пользуется прозой: не догадываясь об этом. Именно поэтому средний ученый сохраняет много привычных, непроницаемых переборок, не ставит тех вопросов, которые вытекают из *общего* движения научной мысли и робко останавливается перед обобщениями, где они требуют диалектического прыжка.

Диалектика не освобождает исследователя от кропотливого изучения фактов, наоборот: обязывает к [*этому*] нему. Но зато она сообщает исследующей мысли [*гибкость*] эластичность, помогает справиться с окостеневшими предрассудками, вооружает ее[9] неоценимыми аналогиями и [*прививает*] воспитывает ее в духе отваги, подкованного осмотрительностью.

    Etonnante découverte d'un savant italien
  Rome, 5 juin.—Une découverte exceptionnellement importante vient d'être faite par l'académicien d'Italie, M. Enrico Fermi.
  Celui-ci est arrivé à créer artificiellement un nouveau corps simple s'ajoutant à la liste des 92 corps simples existants. Ses travaux font suite à ceux des savants français Joliot et Mme Curie. seux-ci, après leur découverte du neutron, étaient parvenus à se servir de ce corpuscule pour "bombarder" le noyau atomique d'un certain nombre de corps simples; le corps simple ainsi bombardé se transformait en un autre corps simple, mais toujours dans la série des corps existants, c'est-à-dire de 1 (hydregène) à 92 (uranium).
  M. Enrico Fermi, par le même procédé, a réussi à bombarder le dernier corps de la série, c'est-à-dire l'atome d'uranium.
  L'éclatement du noyau atomique bombardé a donné naissance à un nouveau corps appelé "élément 93".
  L'annonce de cette découverté a été faite, au cours de la séance de clôture de l'année académique, par le sénateur Mario Orso Corbino.

Пример Менделеева, которому отсутствие диалектического метода помешало признать взаимопревращаемость элементов, несмотря на то, что открытая им периодическая таблица элементов свела качественные различия между ними к количественным различиям атомных весов[.]

---

9. В тексте: "его".

Антиномия: *причина* и *следствие*
(причина и цель) в другом порядке
базис и *надстройка*
"*взаимодействие*":

понимаемое { метафизически и диалектически

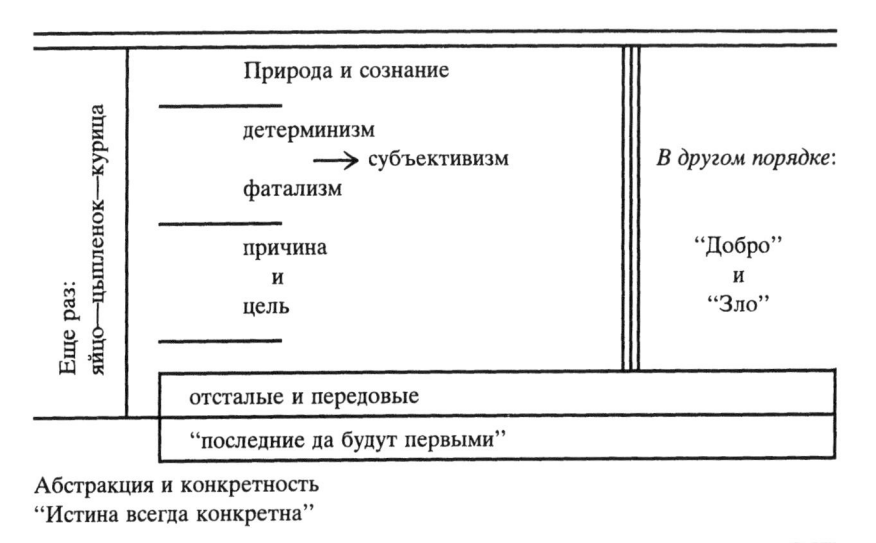

Еще раз: яйцо—цыпленок—курица	Природа и сознание детерминизм ⟶ субъективизм фатализм причина и цель	*В другом порядке*: "Добро" и "Зло"

отсталые и передовые
"последние да будут первыми"

Абстракция и конкретность
"Истина всегда конкретна"

Триада
Тезис—Антитезис—Синтезиз
Отрицание отрицания

Рассудок и разум

Национал-социализм
[*Ленин и Мартов*]

Элементы диалектики проникают в той или иной степени [во] всякое мышление, тем более мышление "цивилизованных" людей нашего времени, переживших величайшие технические преобразования, экономические потрясения, войны и революции. В области идеологической национал-социализм представляет собой крайнюю реакцию против диалектики, более тяжеловесную в своей последовательности, чем итальянский фашизм, насквозь эклектический. Философски национал-социализм направлен не более и не менее, как против идеи развития: он злобно отвергает потому не только марксизм, но и дарвинизм,—он хочет вернуть познание к [*вечным*] незыблемым началам; в [*области*] отношении человеческого общества таким[*и*] категориям[*и*] [*метафизическими (по Гегелю) категориями*] оказываются *раса* и *кровь*. Могущество диалектического мышления доказывает здесь свою силу методом от обратного: последовательная оппозиция против диалектики отбрасывает в глубины Тевтобургского леса.

Ленин и Мартов

Если все современное мышление прошито элементами диалектики, то [*тем более по*] [*заранее ясно, что Мартов, серьезно начитанный марксист*] тем более политическое мышление меньшевиков, прошедших школу марксизма и революционных событий. Но диалектика диалектике рознь. Мартов очень тонко, во многих случаях виртуозно, владел диалектикой. Но это была диалектика близких [*ему*] его мышлению явлений, в среде интеллигенции, связанной с интеллигенцией верхушки рабочих.

Мартов подчас очень [*тонко и*] умно анализировал перегруппировки в сфере парламентской политики, изменения тенденций в прессе, маневры правящих кругов—поскольку все это органичивалось текущей политикой подготовкою к отдаленным событиям или мирными условиями довоенной Европы, когда на политической арене действуют только [*представители*] вожди, депутаты, журналисты, министры, когда основные противники остаются фактически неизменными.

[*Диалектическое мышление есть конкретное*]

В этих пределах Мартов плавал, как рыба в воде. Его диалектика была диалектикой производных процессов и коротких масштабов, эпизодических изменений. За этими пределами он пасовал.

Наоборот, диалектика Ленина имела массивный характер. Его мысль—в этом его нередко обвиняли противники—"упрощала" действительность на самом деле сметала второстепенное и эпизодическое, чтобы оперировать с основным. Так Энгельс "упрощал" действительность, когда определял государство, как вооружен[ные] отряды людей с мат[ериальными] привесками в виде тюрем. Но это было *спасительное* упрощение: недостаточное, правда, само по себе для оценки [*для того, чтоб разобраться в*] конъюнктуры дня, оно решало в последнем историческом счете.

Мысль Ленина оперировала с живыми классами, как с основным фактором общества и потому обнаруживала *всю* силу в такие периоды, когда на сцену вступали большие массы, т.е. в периоды [*больших*] глубоких потрясений, войн и революций. Ленинская диалектика была диалектикой больших масштабов.

Хотя [*общие*] основные законы механики [*общие для всех сфер*] распространяются на всю производственную деятельность человека, на деле есть[10] механика часового мастера и механика Днепростроя. [*Диалектика*] Мысль Мартова была мыслью [*талантливого*] часовых дел мастера в политике. Мысль Ленина жила в масштабах Днепростроя. Различие количественного порядка? [*Не забудем, что*] Количество и здесь переходит в качество.

часов[ой] маст[ер]
колич[ество] здесь пер[еходит] в кач[ество]
Но диалектика малых масштабов зависит от д[иалекти]ки боль[ших] масш[табов]? Когда[11] [. . .]

---

10. В тексте: "на деле но есть".
11. В дневнике Троцкого данный отрывок врезается в текст между словами "перегруппировки в сфере парламентской по-" и "литики, изменения тенденций в прессе". Последнее слово: "ко..."—неразборчиво и может читаться как "конец" или "когда".

Сравнение с часовым мастером имеет, однако, очень условное значение. Часовой механизм живет всегда (пока не испортится) своей "самодовлеющей" жизнью, [*тогда как политика малых масштабов*] и часовая стрелка может правильно показывать час, хотя бы мастер и плохо знал законы движения земли вокруг своей оси. Но политика малых масштабов (внутренние группировки в партиях, парламентская игра и пр.) [*решаются процессами больших масштабов*] сохраняет относительную независимость только до тех пор, пока неподвижны (относительно) большие факторы, т.е. классы. Диалектика Мартова давала потому [*все*] тем более трагические осечки и в малых масштабах [и] вопросах, чем ближе надвигались бурные конфликты классов, [*исторические*] пертурбанции в жизни общества. А так как вся наша эпоха с первых годов столетия стала эпохой все более грандиозных [*войн и революций*] исторических пертурбаций, то мысль Мартова все более обнаруживала свою слабость, превращала диалектику в простое прикрытие внутренней неуверенности подпадала под влияние вульгарных эмпириков, как Дан.

Наоборот, мысль Ленина тем отчетливее анализировала все второстепенные явления, все элементы надстойки, тем непосредственнее становилась их зависимость от пришедших в движение классов. От этапа к этапу мысль Ленина становилась крепче, мужественнее и в то же время тоньше и гибче.

Ошибки Мартова были всегда и неизменно ошибками *вправо* от исторического развития, [они] росли в числе и размере [и] скоро переходили из области тактики в область стратегии и тем самым свели на нет [*всю*] тактическую находчивость и богатство инициативы.

[*Ошибки Ле*]
Политические ошибки Ленина были [*почти*] всегда *влево* от линии развития, причем чем дальше, тем становились [*меньше*] реже, меньше по углу отклонения, тем скорее познавались и исправлялись, тем самым отношение

между стратегией и тактикой достигало все более высокого и совершенного соответствия.

<u>Материалистичшеская диалектика</u>
(начало)

Диалектика есть логика развития. Она рассматривает мир—весь без изъятия—не как результат творения, внезапного возникновения, осуществления плана, а как результат [*возникновения*] движения, преобразования. Все, что есть, *стало* таким, каким оно есть, в результате законообразного развития.

В этом своем основном и самом общем [*и основном*] смысле диалектический взгляд на природу и человека совпадает с т[ак] наз[ываемым] "эволюционным" взглядом современных естественных и общественных наук, поскольку они действительно заслуживают этого имени. Нужно только отметить, что философская концепция развития [*отражающаяся на предшествующем развитии науки и возникновения*] всего существующего, [*опирающаяся на*] представлявшая смелое обобщение предшествующего развития науки, возникла до дарвинизма и марксизма и косвенно или прямо оплодотворила их.

Мы дальше увидим, что "эволюция", как общая формула возникновения мира и общества, более бесформенна, менее конкретна, менее содержательна, чем диалектическая концепция. Сейчас для нас достаточно того, что диалектическая (или эволюционная) точка зрения, последовательно примененная, неотвратимо ведет к материализму: органический мир возник из неорганического; сознание есть [*функция*] способность живых организмов, опирающаяся на эволюционно возникшие органы. Другими словами "душа" эволюции (диалектики) сводится в последнем счете к материи. Последовательно и до конца доведенная точка зрения эволюции не оставляет места ни для идеализма, ни для дуализма, ни для других видов эклектики.

Таким образом, "материалистическая диалектика" (или диалектический материализм") не есть произвольное сочетание двух независимых терминов, а есть расчлененное единство—короткая формула цельного и нераздельного миросозерцания, которое одно только и опирается на все развитие научной мысли во всех разветвлениях, которое одно только служит научной опорой для практики человека.

Либеральное понятие "прогресса"
Вестник Европы, Шестой год, Книга Вторая, февраль 1871
#

Торговые задачи России
Развитие международных торговых связей,—скажем словами Д. С. Милля,—"будучи главной гарантией мира на земном шаре, служат великим, прочным залогом непрерывного прогресса понятий, учреждений и свойств человеческого рода".

Перенести сюда то, что сказано о Клемансо, его отношении к эволюционизму и пр.

Напомнить, как яйца "прогрессируют" в курицу[.]

Старый софизм о лысом человеке есть диалектическое обнаружение несостоятельности (=недостаточности) формальных категорий[.]

В противоположность фотографии, которая есть элемент формальной логики, фильм "диалектичен"
(Плохо выражено)

Познающая мысль начинает с различения, с моментальных фотографий, с установления терминов-понятий, в которые укладываются отдельные моменты процесса, но от к[о]т[о]рых ускользает процесс в целом. Эти термины-понятия, созданные познающей мыслью, [*встают затем перед нею*] превращаются затем для нее в оковы. Диалектика снимает эти оковы, обнаруживая относительность неподвижных понятий, их переход друг в друга (S.Logik, I, S. 26–27).

"Мы можем исследовать реальность и без диалектики".

Так же, как мы можем ходить без анатомии и переваривать без физиологии[.]

Абсолютный идеализм Гегеля направлен против дуализма—против вещи в себе (I, 28). Не есть ли признание реальности внешнего мира, *вне* познающего сознания и независимо от него, возвращение[12] к дуализму? Ни в каком случае, ибо познание для нас не самостоятельное начало, а [*часть*] специализованная часть объективного мира (уточнить).

Эволюционная точка зрения вовсе не врождена нашему разуму (Энгельс). Поэтому эволюционной логике (диалектике) надо *учиться*. Истман издевается над этими.

[*Если б человечество*] Разум, который присутствовал бы при дальнейшей эволюции земли, при возникновении солнечной системы и затем при развитии на ней органической жизни и пр. и способен был бы охватить эти процессы, был бы, [*конечно*] так сказать[,] имманентно от рождения диалектическим разумом. Но наш человеческий разум является последышем природы. На памяти человечества природа давала не столько картину изменен[ий], сколько повторяющихся круговращений. "Возвращается ветер на круги своя". Само человечество есть последовательная смена поколений[.] Каждое поколение [*познает*] начинает трудную работу познания в известном смысле сначала. В пределах повседневной практики человек привык иметь дело с неизменными [*величинами*] объектами. В результате этого врожденной, унаследованной, автоматизированной является рассудочная логика, которая расчленяет природу на само-

---

12. В тексте: "возвращению".

стоятельные и неизменные элементы. Только на основе накопленного научного опыта под толчками исторического (классового) развития мысль прокладывает себе дорогу от вульгарной логики к диалектике[.]

Рационализм есть попытка на основе вульгарной логики создать законченную систему[.]

/*Хронология эволюционизма*
Канто-*лаплассовская* теория возникновения солнечной системы
Диалектика Г е г е л я[14] (после французской революции)
Теория Лайеля (эволюция земли)
Теория Маркса/[13]

Таким образом, [*последовательный*] переход от мышления в неподвижных категориях, к мышлению в развитии ведет свое происхождение от эпохи после Вел. Ф. Рев.,[15] которая была последней великой гениальной вспышкой мужественного рационализма.

Кант[16] видит раннее совершенство *логики* в том, что со времени *Аристотеля,* т.е. в течение двух тысяч лет, она не подверглась изменению.

Гегель, наоборот, видит в этом величайшую отсталость логики.

Суть в том, что правила и приемы узко-практического обыденного или вульгарного мышления кристаллизовались—на основе всей практики—и связанной с нею теоретической работы—очень рано, еще в дверности, и в рамках этого обыденного мышления не требовали и не терпели изменения. Но именно рост и развитие познания на основах Аристотелевой логики подготовляли ее взрыв[.]

---

13. Текст, взятый в косые скобки, в оригинале обведен красным карандашом.
14. Слово "Гегеля" написано красным карандашом.
15. Великой французской революции.
16. Слова "Кант", "Аристотеля" и "Гегель" в оригинале написаны красным карандашом.

Триада есть "механика" превращения количества в качество

Исторически человек формирует свои "понятия"—основные элементы своего мышления—на основе опыта, всегда неполного, частичного, одностороннего. Он включает в [*изолированное, замкнутое*] "понятие" те черты живого вечно меняющегося процесса, которые важны и значительны для него в данный момент. Его дальнейший опыт сперва обогащает (количественно), а затем *перерастает* замкнутое понятие, т.е. практически отрицает его, вынуждая тем самым к теоретическому отрицанию. Но отрицание не означает возвращения назад к tabula rasa. Разум уже обладает а) "понятием" и б) признанием его несостоятельности. Это признание равносильно необходимости строить *новое понятие,* причем неизбежно обнаруживается, что отрицание было не абсолютным, что оно распространялось только на определенные черты первого понятия. Новое понятие имеет поэтому по необходимости *синтетический* характер: в него входят те элементы исходного понятия, которые выдержали испытания опыта + те новые элементы опыта, которые привели к отрицанию исходного понятия.

Так и в области мышления (познания) количественные изменения приводят к качественным, причем эти превращения имеют не незаметно-"эволюционный" характер, а сопровождаются *перерывами постепенности,* т.е. малыми или большими умственными катастрофами. В сумме это и значит, что развитие познания имеет *диалектический характер*[.]

Новое "синтетическое" понятие в свою очередь становится исходным моментом для нового опыта, обогащения, проверки и для нового *отрицания*. Таково место триады в развитии человеческой мысли. *Но каково ее место в развитии природы?*[17]

---

17. Подчеркнуто красным карандашом.

Здесь мы подходим к важнейшему вопросу диалектической философии.

Взаимоотношение между сознанием (познанием) и природой есть самостоятельная область со своими закономерностями[.]

Сознание дробит природу на неподвижные категории и тем вступает в противоречие с реальностью. Диалектика преодолевает это противоречие—постепенно и по частям—приближая сознание к реальности мира. Диалектика сознания (познания) не есть таким образом *отражение* диалектики природы, а есть *результат* активного взаимодействия между сознанием и природой и—вместе с тем—метод познания, вытекающий из этого взаимодействия.

Как познание не *тождественно* с миром (вопреки идеалистическому постулату Гегеля), так и диалектика познания не *тождественна* с диалектикой природы. Сознание представляет своеобразную *часть* природы, имеющую такие особенности и закономерности, которых совершенно лишена вся остальная природа. Субъективная диалектика должна тем самым представлять своеобразную часть объективной диалектики—со своими особыми формами и закономерностями. (Опасность состоит в перенесении—под видом "объективизма"—родовых мук, спазм сознания на объективную природу.[)]

Диалектика познания приближает сознание к "тайнам" природы, т.е. помогает овладевать и диалектикой природы. Но в чем состоит *диалектика* природы? Где грань, отделяющая ее от диалектики познания (зыбкая, диалектическая "грань")[.]

Сознание дейтсвует, как фотогр[афический] аппарат: оно вырывает у природы "моменты" и теряет между ними связь и переходы. Но объект фотографии, живой человек, не разбивается на моменты. Уже кинематогр[афическая] лента дает нам грубую "непрерывность", удовлетворительную для сетчатки нашего глаза и приближающуюся к непрерывности природы. Правда, кинем[атографиче]ская непрерывность состоит на самом деле из отдельных "моментов" и коротких перерывов между ними. Но и то, и другое относится к технике кинематографа, эксплоатирующего несовершенство глаза.

Проверить, как эта проблема трактуется у Ленина и Плеханова.

Гегель сам говорил не раз о необходимой конкретности, вытекающей из имманентного движения "моментов"—движения, которое представляет прямую противоположность аналитического подхода (Verfahrens), т.е. действия, внешнего по отношению к самому предмету (Sache), и свойственного субъекту (I, 60)[.]

22/VI 1934

Тождество *Бытия* (Sein) и *Ничто* (Nichts), как и противоречивость понятия Начало, в котором объединяются Nichts и Sein, кажется на первый взгляд тонкой, но бесплодной игрой мысли. На самом деле эта "игра" гениально обнаруживает несостоятельность статического мышления, которое сперва дробит мир на неподвижные элементы, а затем ищет истины путем беспредельного расширения пр[оцесса.]

Роль эмигрантов

Вся информация о Западе, в том числе и через легальную печать (вплоть до либеральной)[,] шла через них.

Легальный и нелегальный марксизм
1905

Легальные писатели царской России не только не всё высказывали, но и не всё додумывали. В сущности они не досказывали и часто не додумывали самого главного. Оставаясь в рамках легальности[,] они выхолащивали свою мысль. Нелегальная печать казалась им "упрощенной", "фанатической", "прямолинейной". Но когда наступили "дни свободы", оказалось, что полем журналистики овладели подпольщики, эмигранты. Только они умели писать на языке революции. Но этого мало: именно из эмиграции пришли наиболее талантливые журналисты. Не случайно: политика требует темперамента, последовательности, мужества, и эти качества находят свое выражение и в стиле.

Тождество противоположностей
Маленький Paul говорит "donne!" и тогда, когда хочет взять, и тогда, когда хочет дать.

Le troisième centenaire
du "Discours de la Méthode"

Nous avons recu le lettre suivante:
Monsieur le directeur,
Le *Temps* du 13 février et celui du 15 ont signalé plusieurs des manifestations qui auront lieu, en 1937, en l'honneur de Descartes. Il intéressera peut-être vos lecteurs de savoir que, cette même année, les philosophes du monde entier, réunis au Palais des congrès de la future Exposition, commémoreront le troisième centenaire du *Discours de la Méthode*. Ainsi en a décidé le huitième congrès international de philosophie, réuni à Prague en 1934; le neuvième congrès aura lieu à Paris en 1937, et sera un "Congrès Descartes"; en liaison avec le commission Descartes, présidée par M. Paul Valéry, les organisateurs de ce congrès préparent un programme qui illustrera les aspects universels de la pensée de Descartes.

Veuillez agréer, monsieur le directeur, l'assurance de mes sentiments de haute considération.
Emile Bréhier,
professeur à la Sorbonne.

Почему на известном этапе развития научной мысли в разных областях приходится ставить теорию "на ноги" (предполагая, что она стояла до этого на голове)?

Потому что человек в своей практич[еской] деятельности сможет рассматривать весь мир, как средство, [*для цели человека*] а себя, как цель. Пратический эгоцентризм (homo-центризм) [*опрокидывает*]—перенесенный в теорию—опрокидывает все мироздание на голову. Отсюда необходимость "поправки" (Кант-Лапласс, Лайель, Дарвин, Маркс)[.]

Мозг есть материальный субстрат сознания. Значит ли это, что сознание есть просто форма "проявления" физиологических процессов в мозгу? Если б дело обстояло так, то пришлось бы спросить: к чему же понадобилось сознание? Если сознание не имеет никакой *самостоятельной* функции, поднимающейся *над* физиологическими процессами в мозгу и нервах, то оно не нужно,[18] бесполезно, оно вредно, так как представляет лишнее усложение,—и какое!

Наличность сознания и его увенчания, логической мыслью,[19] может быть биологически и социально "оправдана" только в том случае, если оно дает положительные жизненные результаты сверх тех, какие достигаются системой бессознательных [*и подсознательных*] рефлексов. Это предполагает не только независимость сознания (в известных пределах) от "автоматических" процессов в мозгу и нервах, но и способность сознания воздействовать на действия и функции тела. Каковы же рычаги, служащие сознанию для достижения этих целей? Эти рычаги явно не могут иметь материальный характер, [*ибо в этих случаях*] иначе они включились бы в цепь анатомно-физиологических процессов организма и не могли бы играть самостоятельной роли, составляющей их значение и функцию. Мысль оперирует по своим собственным законам, которые мы можем назвать законами логики, приходя при их помощи к известным практическим выводам, она включает последние (с большим или меньшим успехом) в цепь нашей жизнедеятельности.

Существует, как известно, целая школа психиатрии ("психоанализм" Фрейда), которая практически совершенно абстрагируется от физиологии, опираясь на внутренний детерминизм психических явлений, как таковых. Некоторые

---

18. В тексте: "ненужно".
19. В тексте: "мысли".

[*"материалисты"*] критики обвиняют, поэтому, школу Фрейда в идеализме. Что [*некоторые*] [*многие*] психоаналитики нередко склонны к дуализму, идеализму и мистицизму. Так, Fr. Wittels (Freud, l'homme, la doctrine, l'école), франц[узский] перевод, упрекает своего учителя в том, что тот не [*осмелился*] дерзнул "dépouiller complètement l'âme de tout ce qui est organique" (207). Это, насколько я знаю, факт. Но сам по себе метод психоанализа, исходящий из "автономности" психических явлений, нисколько не противоречит материализму[.] Наоборот, именно диалектический материализм и подсказывает нам ту мысль, что психика не могла бы даже и сформироваться, если б она не играла [*самостоятельной*] автономной, т.е. в известных пределах самостоятельной роли в жизни [*организма*] индивида и рода.

Но все же мы подходим здесь к какому-то критическому пункту, к перерыву постепенности, к переходу количества в качество: психика, возникшая из материи, "освобождается" от детерминизма материи для того, чтоб [*в свою очередь*] самостоятельно—по своими собственным законам—воздействовать на материю.

Правда, диалектика причин и следствий, базиса и надстройки не новость для нас: политика вырастает из экономики, чтоб в свою очередь воздействовать на базу рычагами надстроенного характера. Но здесь взаимоотношения представляются реальные, ибо действуют в обоих случаях живые люди: в одном случае они группируются для производства, в другом они под давлением нужд того же производства группируются политически и воздействуют рычагами политики на собственную производственную группировку.

Когда мы от анатомии и физиологии мозга переходим к умственной деятельности, взаимоотношение "базиса" и "надстройки" представляется несравненно загадочнее.

Дуалисты делят мир на самостоятельные субстанции: материю и сознание. Куда девать при этом бессознательное?

6. Russian Text of the Additional Notes

Диалектика

Сил[л]огизм безусловно правилен только тогда, когда он—тавтология, т.е. когда он бесплоден.

Силлогизм "полезен" тогда, когда он . . . не правилен, т.е. когда он допускает в понятиях "зазор"[.]

Все дело в допустимых размерах "зазора". Здесь и начинается диалектика[.]

Основной "клеточкой" диалект[ического] мышления является силлогизм. Но он сам деформируется, изменяется, как изменяется основная клеточка в разных тканях организма[.]

"Философия = инструментальный цех по отношению ко всем остальным цехам науки[.]

Инструментальный цех не заменяет всего производства. Что[бы] пользовать[ся] инструментом надо знать специальное производств[о] (слесарное, токарное). Когда невежда, вооружен[ный] "матер[иалистической] диалектикой"[,] пытается разрешать по наитию сложные специальные вопросы, то он неизбежно оказывается в дураках[.]

С другой сторо[ны],

"Цеховой" ученый может обходиться и без инструментального цела, т.е. может пользоваться самодельным инструментом, но его работа от его явно пострадает (Дарвин, Менделеев и п[р.])[.]

"Наша рев[олюция]." 1906 г.
от Клячко

Философию Гегеля Герцен называл алгеброй революции.

Диалектика есть логика развития. Логика (формальн[ая]) есть диалектика неподвижности[.]

Логика есть частный случай диалектики, когда движение и изменение входит в формулу нулем.

Цицерон считал, что между бесспорно достоверным и бесспорно ложным пролегает широкая средняя область, истины которой зависят[1] от субъекта, от того, кто рассуждает: ista sunt ut disputantur

(дословный перевод невозможен)
зависит от точки зрения[.]

"Инженер" играет в социальных построениях М. Истмана и других американцев ту же универсальную роль, какую в построениях старых [*англо-саксонских*] буржуазных политико-экономов играл Робинзон Крузо.

Люди относятся к идеям двояко: либо как к произвольной внереальной тени, стоящей вне мира фактов в их материальной обусловленности, либо как ко всемогущему "фактору", который командует реальностью. Оба отношения ложны. Идея есть факт в цепи других фактов[.]

"У Гегеля диалектика стоит на голове. Надо ее поставить на ноги, чтобы вскрыть рациональное зерно под мистической оболочкой", эти слова Маркса из предисловия ко второму изданию ["]Капитала["] (1873 г.) давали не раз пищу для изощрения критического остроумия.

Но в сущности ту же операцию—опрокидывания с го-

---

1. Так в тексте. По смыслу должно быть: "область истины, которая зависит".

ловы на ноги—приходилось повторять во всех областях человеческой мысли.

Бог создал человека[.]
Человек создал бога.

———

Земля вращается вокруг солнца[.]
Солнце вращается вокруг земли.

———

ДИАЛЕКТИКА

"Опрокинуть на голову . . ." Издевательства над этим (Истман)[.] Между тем наука, как и искусство, полны такими опрокидывания[ми] на голову.

2.[2] До-дарвинновская биология установила целесообразность структуры видов, соотвествие органов и условия жизни. Отсюда она заключала к предвзятой системе. Дарвин не отверг "целесообразность", как соответствие органов, функций и среды, но опрокинул взаимозависимость на голову. В этом гениальном опрокидывании и лежит суть дарвинизма[.]

К этому приурочить цитаты о дарвинизме.

1. Космология до Галилея установила взаимозависимость между движениями солнца и земли. Галилей не отверг этой зависимости, но опрокинул ее на голову.

3. Менделеев и его периодическая система элементов. Для него неразложимые индивидуальности стали в известное математич[еское] отношение друг другу. Дальнейшее развитие химии опрокинуло это взаимоотношение на голову.

Вся эволюция есть переход количества в качество. Самое понятие постепенного медленного развития и означает достижение качественных ценностей при помощи количественных изменний. Это относится решительно ко всем областям.

Естественный отбор Дарвина, ведущий к созданию

---

2. Цифры написаны цветным карандашом.

разных растительных и животных видов, есть ни что иное, как накопление количественных изменений, дающих в результате новые качества, новый вид.

Кто отрицает диалектический закон перехода количества в качество, тот должен отрицать генетическое единство растительных и животных видов, химических элементов и пр. Тот должен, в конце концов, вернуться к библейскому акту творения.

Телеологическое мышление

Толстой не хотел допустить, что он существует на земле без заранее данной цели, как выпавший из гнезда птенец[.]

"Важно то, чтоб признать бога хозяином и знать, чего он от меня требует; а что он сам такое, и как он живет, я никогда не узнаю, потому что я ему не пара. Я работник, он хозяин[.]" (Толстой)

Телеология и детерминизм

Все школы субъективизма так или иначе опираются на противоречия объективной причины и субъективной цели. Детерминизм есть философия объективных причинностей. Телеология есть философия субъективных целей. Попытка противопоставить их враждебно или эклектически сочетать их представляет собой продукт философского невежества. Цель есть частный вид причины. Телеология есть только особый отдел детерминизма.

Дарвинизм

Все признавали процесс образования *разновидностей* путем естественного или искусственного отбора, но многие категорически отказывались признать тот же процес[с] для образования *видов*. До тех пор, пока переходные формы налицо[,] единство вида кажется незыблемым. Но исчезают переходные формы между разновидностями, и разновидности становятся видами.—[Каждый процесс имеет свою материальную или нематериальную палеонтологию.][3]

---

3. Квадратные скобки Троцкого.

Учение Дарвина из теории происхождения видов стало теорией эволюции органического мира.

Зоологическая география Дарвина и Уоллеса—благодаря эвол[юционной] теори[и] отделена пропастью от зоогеографии Линнея и пр. (Роль палеонтологии)[.]

Вымершие посредствующие звенья.

История языка—палеонтология мысли[.]

По какой линии шли *возражения против дарвинизма?* Голландский ботаник де Фриз, автор так называемой мутационной теории, пробовал установить *принципиальное* различие между особенностями разновидностей и особенностями вида, тем самым непереходность одних в другие. (Но де Фриз все же эволюционист)[.]

До Дарвина вопрос о происхождении видов почитался "тайной из тайн"[.]

Уоллес о Дарвине:

"У меня нет . . . того неутомимого терпенья при собирании многочисленных, самых разнообразных фактов, той удивительной способности выводить заключения, тех точных и богатых физиологических познаний, того остроумия при определении плана опытов и той ловкости при их выполнении, наконец, того бесподобного слога—ясного и в то же время убедительного и точного,—словом всех тех качеств, которые делают из Дарвина человека совершенного . . ."

(применить к характеристике Ленина—показать однородность качеств в разных областях)

Диалектика

Уоллес—не только дарвинист, но ученый, самостоятельно дошедши[й] до учения об эволюционном происхождении видов (в том числе и человека) потратил не мало сил на доказательство непроходимой грани между человеком и животными в области умств[енной] и нравств[енной], другими словами на доказательство божественного происхождения "души".

Такие же скачки делает Уоллес в отношении перехода от неорган[ической] к органич[еской] материи и появления сознания[.]

———

Эволюция не допускает сделок: надо либо признать, либо отвергнуть ее[.]

Всякая реакция должна отвергать *трансформизм*
Национал-социализм непримирим с дарвинизмом

Notes

1. Notes on Lenin and Revolutionary Politics

1. Letter from Trotsky to Max Eastman (undated, probably summer 1929), Trotsky Collection, Lilly Library, Indiana University; letter from Trotsky to Eastman, June 13, 1929, in the same archive.

2. Much of the Trotsky-Eastman correspondence is devoted to Trotsky's troubles with publishers and his suspicions about them. He was convinced that Schumann, the German publisher with whom he had signed a contract in March 1929, had dealings with Stalin's agents. Trotsky took Schumann to court in order to dissolve the contract and won his case in Berlin in February 1930. Then, in December 1931 Trotsky dissolved his agreement with Charles Boni, for whom he had been writing *The History of the Russian Revolution,* and with Eastman's help placed the book with Simon and Schuster. Letters from Trotsky to Eastman, February 24, 1930, December 11, 1931, and others. Trotsky Collection, Lilly Library, Indiana University.

3. Letter from Trotsky to Eastman, January 2, 1931, Trotsky Collection, Lilly Library, Indiana University.

4. See Carlo Sforza, *Makers of Modern Europe* (Indianapolis: Bobbs-Merrill, 1930), ch. 36.

5. Letter from Trotsky to Eastman (undated, probably summer 1929), cited in note 1.

6. Trotsky Collection, Lilly Library, Indiana University.

7. Trotsky, *Portraits, Personal and Political,* George Breitman and George Saunders, eds. (New York: Pathfinder Press, 1977); in addition, see the Russian language edition with additional materials: Trotsky, *Portrety,* Y. Felshtinsky, ed. (Benson, Vt.: Chalidze, 1984).

8. Trotsky, *Trotsky's Diary in Exile, 1935,* E. Zarudnaia, tr. (Cambridge: Harvard University Press, 1976), p. 46.

9. Trotsky, *The History of the Russian Revolution,* Max Eastman, tr. (Ann Arbor: University of Michigan Press, 1932), 3 vols., 1:329–30.

10. Isaac Deutscher, *The Prophet Outcast* (New York: Oxford University Press, 1980), p. 246. For a commentary on Deutscher as well as Trotsky, see Baruch Knei-Paz, *The Social and Political Thought of Leon Trotsky* (Oxford: Clarendon, 1978), pp. 510–32. For a defense of Trotsky's position in the Deutscher-Trotsky split, see George Novack,

Understanding History (New York: Pathfinder Press, 1972), pp. 71–81. Novack criticizes both Deutscher and Sidney Hook, who had reviewed *The Prophet Outcast*.

11. Trotsky, *Stalin: An Appraisal of the Man and His Influence*, Charles Malamuth, ed. and tr. (New York: Harper, 1941), p. 205.

12. Trotsky Archives, T3809, Houghton Library, Harvard University. "Predislovie" ("Foreword"). The notes are handwritten, in ink, on standard size typing paper. Some of the sheets in the folder are cut, some pasted together. All the notes are in Trotsky's hand.

13. Deutscher, *The Prophet Outcast*, p. 260.

14. Natalia Sedov Trotsky, "Father and Son," in *Leon Trotsky: The Man and His Work*, Joseph Hansen et al., eds. (New York: Merit, 1969), p. 43.

15. Trotsky, *Trotsky's Diary*, p. 66.

16. The English version that will be cited here is L. Trotsky, *The Young Lenin*, Max Eastman, tr. (Garden City, N.Y.: Doubleday, 1972). For foreign language texts, see Louis Sinclair, *Leon Trotsky: A Bibliography* (Stanford: Hoover Institution Press, 1972), p. 553.

17. Those speeches, essays, and articles that tended in this direction and contributed to the growing cult of Lenin are cited in N. Tumarkin, *Lenin Lives! The Lenin Cult in Soviet Russia* (Cambridge: Harvard University Press, 1983); in addition, Knei-Paz has commented on the uneven character of Trotsky's comments on Lenin, but probably misjudges Trotsky's state of mind, which he characterizes as "almost hysterical," when referring to one of the sketches, in *The Social and Political Thought of Leon Trotsky*, pp. 522–23, n. 91.

18. L. Trotsky, *On Lenin*, Tamara Deutscher, tr. (London: Harrap, 1971), p. 101. Trotsky later embellished this account with the obvious intention of showing that he could be right and Lenin wrong—that their roles were at times reversed. See, for example, Trotsky, *My Life* (New York: Pathfinder Press, 1970), pp. 455–60.

19. Trotsky, *My Life*, p. 287.

20. Trotsky, *The History of the Russian Revolution*, 1:95.

21. Trotsky Archives, T3809. The references are to Emil Ludwig and André Maurois (E. S. W. Herzog).

22. Trotsky Archives, bMsRuss13.3, H17 (1 of 2). The translation of these notes is Charles Malamuth's.

23. Trotsky, *Stalin*, p. 270.

24. *Ibid.*, p. 373.

25. Sergei Nechaev (1847–1882) had collaborated with Bakunin on the composition of "The Catechism of a Revolutionary" in 1869. He brutally murdered one of his own followers later that year. The transcript of the trial of his revolutionary organization inspired Dostoevsky to write *The Possessed*.

26. Trotsky, *Stalin*, pp. 104–6.

27. Trotsky Archives, T3785 (1 of 3, last typed page).

28. Trotsky, *The Young Lenin*, p. 203.

29. Trotsky Archives, T3785 (first paragraph in 1 of 3; second in 3 of 3).

30. Trotsky Archives, T4759, "Rezhim Stalina, Partiia," pp. 2–3.

31. See Isaac Deutscher, *The Prophet Armed* (New York: Oxford University Press, 1980), pp. 420, 426.

32. In "Rezhim Stalina, Partiia," Trotsky used the word "apparat" instead of "organizatsiia" when quoting his own words of 1904. This, of course, is a retrospective editing. T4759, p. 8.

Notes: Dialectics

33. *Ibid.*
34. *Ibid.*, pp. 8–9.
35. *Ibid.*, pp. 9–10.
36. Trotsky, *Trotsky's Diary in Exile*, pp. 165–67.
37. Trotsky, *My Life*, p. 184.

2. Notes on Dialectics and Evolutionism

1. This is based on a conversation with Mr. van Heijenoort. The regimen followed by Trotsky and his household in exile is described in greater detail in van Heijenoort's book *With Trotsky in Exile* (Cambridge: Harvard University Press, 1978), pp. 13–18; the period of exile in France is described in chapter 2. In addition, van Heijenoort gives a description in the collection *Leon Trotsky: The Man and His Works,* Joseph Hansen et al., eds. (New York: Merit, 1969), p. 45; another appears by Charles Cornell in the same collection, p. 65.

2. Isaac Deutscher, *The Prophet Armed* (New York: Oxford University Press, 1980), pp. 38–39; Trotsky, *My Life* (New York: Pathfinder Press, 1970), ch. 8.

3. The following are relevant: "A Letter to Academician I. P. Pavlov" (September 27, 1923); "To the First All-Russian Congress of Scientific Workers" (November 24, 1923); "D. I. Mendeleev and Marxism" (September 17, 1925). They are found in the section "Science and Revolution" in Trotsky's *Sochineniia*, series 6, *Problems of Culture,* A. Osher, Ia. Renzin, and I. Rumer, eds. (Moscow: Gosudarstvennoe izd., 1927), 21:260–88. In addition, see "Radio, Science, Technology, and Society" (March 1, 1926); and the first two parts of "Culture and Socialism" (February 3, 1926), on pp. 410–32 of the same volume. For English translations of all but the first item, see Trotsky, *Problems of Everyday Life* (New York: Pathfinder Press, 1973).

4. Trotsky, *In Defense of Marxism* (New York: Pathfinder Press, 1973), especially the essay "A Petty-Bourgeois Opposition in the Socialist Workers Party," pp. 3–54; and "An Open Letter to Comrade Burnham," pp. 72–94. In addition, a fragment on dialectics and the immutability of the syllogism, apparently intended as part of "A Petty-Bourgeois Opposition," was published among several unfinished works in Trotsky, *Writings of Leon Trotsky, 1939–40* (New York: Pathfinder Press, 1973), pp. 399–405. Here Trotsky refutes the idea that the syllogism's durability resides in an agreement to make it a rule and ridicules the idea as an intellectual version of the social contract. Trotsky proposed instead that the syllogism is a natural way of thinking, an evolutionary endowment found even among animals—an idea to which he returned repeatedly in his work on dialectics and which can be found in the notebooks as well. In the fragment on dialectics he also ridicules Oxford empiricism and the prejudice of empiricists against dialectics. Trotsky rescued the great English thinkers by attributing to them a "primitive form of dialectical thinking." He not only viewed thinking, both syllogistic and dialectical, as evolutionary products, but assumed that creative thinkers had to violate the syllogism. As shall be seen, Trotsky made transgression an essential aspect of creative thought. The notebooks help to clarify these ideas.

5. Trotsky, *In Defense of Marxism*, p. 191.

6. Trotsky, *Trotsky's Diary in Exile, 1935,* E. Zarudnaia, ed. (Cambridge: Harvard University Press, 1976), p. 109.

7. G. A. Ziv, *Trotskii* (New York: Narodopravstvo, 1921), p. 10.

8. Trotsky kept a great many clippings from scientific articles in his archives. They attest to his interest in Darwinism, genetics, physics, and other topics in the natural sciences. Trotsky read the science column of the *New York Times* and the *feuilleton* section of *Le Temps*. He had collected Russian materials from journals such as *Vestnik Evropy, Russkaia mysl', Zhizn'*, and *Otechestvennye zapiski*—all of which had published interesting articles on Darwinism by such distinguished figures as K. Timiriazev, F. Fetter, and N. Mikhailovskii. Trotsky Archives, Houghton Library, Harvard University, T3749.

9. *Materialism and Empirio-Criticism* appeared in 1909; the *Philosophical Notebooks*, although written mainly from 1914 to 1915 were not published during Lenin's lifetime. They appeared as a separate volume for the first time in 1933. Trotsky had in his possession volumes 1–17 of *Leninskii sbornik* (except for volume 14) and a copy of *Materialism and Empirio-Criticism*. It is possible to make at least a rough guess about Trotsky's collection of books on dialectics and related topics at the time when he was writing the notebooks. He had drawn up and dated "February 13, 1934" a bibliography for his book on Lenin, and it is preserved in his archives (Trotsky Archives, T3487).

10. For example, Lenin also liked to scatter comments of approval or disapproval in several languages throughout his notes, "Sehr gut!" common among them. Like Lenin, Trotsky also made frequent use of NB (*nota bene*).

11. Lenin's notes on Hegel's *Wissenschaft der Logik* take up pages 87–215 of volume 29 of the fifth edition of his collected works in Russian.

12. In his autobiography Trotsky wrote: "The brilliant dilettantism of his [Labriola's] exposition actually concealed a profound insight.... Although thirty years [1898–1929] have gone by since I read his essays, the general trend of his argument is still firmly entrenched in my memory, together with his continuous refrain of 'ideas do not drop from the sky.'" Trotsky, *My Life*, p. 119.

13. Isaac Deutscher, *The Prophet Outcast* (New York: Oxford University Press, 1980), p. 267.

14. Trotsky, *Trotsky's Diary in Exile*, p. 119.

15. Baruch Knei-Paz, *The Social and Political Thought of Leon Trotsky* (Oxford: Clarendon, 1978), p. 476, fn. 122.

16. Trotsky, *Trotsky's Diary in Exile*, p. 119.

17. The final entry in the notebook is in ink, whereas the remainder of the notebook is written in pencil. It is perhaps the most interesting entry in the notebooks, despite Trotsky's complaint of illness in his diary entry of May 16, 1935, and he makes a curious remark: "Of course the curve may yet take a temporary turn upward. But in general I have a feeling that liquidation is approaching" (p. 119). It hardly seems accidental that Trotsky was reading about Freud and thinking about the relationship between the human mind and physiology during one of his recurring "cryptogenic" illnesses.

18. This quarrel has been examined by two students of Eastman and the U.S. left—William O'Neill, *The Last Romantic: A Life of Max Eastman* (New York: Oxford University Press, 1978); and John P. Diggins, *Up from Communism* (New York: Harper and Row, 1975).

19. The correspondence is preserved, largely in Eastman's papers in the Lilly Library of Indiana University, but additional materials can be found in the Trotsky Archives.

20. O'Neill, *The Last Romantic*, pp. 125–30.

21. Max Eastman, *Marx and Lenin: The Science of Revolution* (New York: Boni, 1927), pp. 32, 35.

Notes: Dialectics 161

22. *Ibid.*, pp. 113–14.
23. *Ibid.*, pp. 115–16.
24. O'Neill, *The Last Romantic*, p. 129.
25. *Ibid.*
26. See, for example, "Dialectics and the Immutability of Logic," in Trotsky, *Writings of Leon Trotsky, 1939–40*, pp. 399–405.
27. I have been able to verify this by checking the published version against the notes, which have been preserved with Eastman's correspondence with Trotsky in the Lilly Library of Indiana University. Aside from some minor changes in wording, the original manuscript contains the adjective "strong" instead of "robust," immediately followed by "not altogether masculine," and the sentence "I wonder about Lenin." These were deleted and did not appear in the published memoirs. In the original manuscript Eastman did not give the precise physical description of Trotsky's rage that appears in the published memoirs. He simply wrote: "Yesterday we reached a point of tension in our argument about dialectic that was extreme. Intellectual wrath is a description of it" (Trotsky Collection, "Two impressions after living three days in Trotsky's house," July 10, 1932, pp. 1–2). In notes written eight days later, after his departure from Prinkipo, Eastman added, "He was almost hysterical—was actually gasping for breath—when he found himself unable to overpower me with the usual clichés within which the idea of dialectic evolution is defended" (*ibid.*, p. 5). I present the published version in the text. For Eastman's overview of his own career, including his relationship with Trotsky and excerpts from their correspondence see Max Eastman, *Love and Revolution* (New York: Random House, 1964).
28. M. Eastman, *Einstein, Trotsky, Hemingway, Freud, and Other Great Companions* (New York: Collier, 1962), p. 113. Eastman's testimony is reinforced by that of George Novack, a disciple of Trotsky who wrote several books explicating and continuing Trotsky's dialectics. Novack describes a meeting with Trotsky on January 10, 1937, just after Trotsky had arrived in Mexico. When the discussion turned to Max Eastman Trotsky "became tense, agitated." He told Novack (who, ironically, was with Max Shachtman—soon to become a renegade himself): " 'You comrades must at once take up the struggle against Eastman's distortions and repudiation of dialectical materialism . . .' I was somewhat surprised at the vehemence of his argumentation in this matter at such a moment." G. Novack, "Trotsky's Views on Dialectical Materialism," in *Leon Trotsky: The Man and His Work*, p. 94. Novack's relationship with Trotsky evidently also gave him insight into the importance of the idea of the unconscious in Trotsky's vision. See *ibid.*, p. 102.
29. Trotsky to Eastman, November 6, 1933, Trotsky Archives.
30. Max Eastman, *Stalin's Russia and the Crisis of Socialism* (New York: Norton, 1940), p. 124, fn. Eastman was having some fun at Trotsky's expense here, for he knew very well that the accusation of "administrative" rule echoed Lenin's criticism of Trotsky in Lenin's "Testament."
31. For example, see Trotsky, letter of January 4, 1933, to the editorial board of the *Militant* in *Writings of Leon Trotsky, 1932–33*, p. 68.
32. Max Eastman, *Leon Trotsky: The Portrait of a Youth* (New York: Greenberg, 1925), pp. 116–17. See also Trotsky, *Sochineniia*, 21:332–33.
33. Trotsky, *Sochineniia*, 20:118.
34. Trotsky Archives, T3749. The excerpt is from the published correspondence of Aksel'rod and Plekhanov.
35. Trotsky, *Portraits, Personal and Political*, George Breitman and George Saunders, eds. (New York: Pathfinder Press, 1977), p. 30. Trotsky's interpretation of Darwin

was an early form of neo-Darwinian evolutionism, in that it emphasized leaps rather than "insensible variations." "Catastrophism" is currently enjoying a vogue in evolutionary thought. In an interesting survey of early Marxist strategies for rendering Darwin dialectical, Diane B. Paul presents a good statement of the problem posed by Darwin's acceptance of the maxim *natura non facit saltum*. She characterizes Trotsky's interpretation of Darwin as a misunderstanding. See "Marxism, Darwinism, and the Theory of Two Sciences," *Marxist Perspectives* (Spring 1979), 2:120–22.

36. N. Bukharin, *Historical Materialism* (New York: International Publishers, 1925), pp. 81–82.

37. Trotsky, *Sochineniia*, 21:333.

38. In the article on Kautsky cited above, he described social change in these terms: "Marx's theory of the historical process encompasses the entire history of human social organization. But in ages of relative social equilibrium the fact that ideas depend upon class interests and the property system remains masked. The age of revolution is Marxism's school of advanced study. Then the struggle of classes resulting from systems of property assumes the character of open civil war" (Trotsky, *Portraits,* p. 30).

39. See, for example, Trotsky, "A Letter to Academician I. P. Pavlov," *Sochineniia,* 21:260; "Culture and Socialism," *Sochineniia,* 20:430; and a speech given in Copenhagen on November 27, 1932, Trotsky Archives, T3469–72 (four versions).

40. Trotsky, *Sochineniia,* 21:430.

41. Trotsky, *Sochineniia,* 21:268–88.

42. Letter from Trotsky to James Burnham, April 18, 1938, in Trotsky Archives; see also Louis Sinclair, *Leon Trotsky: A Bibliography* (Stanford: Hoover Institution Press, 1972), p. 380.

43. Most notable is Trotsky's sense of levels of organization—of the emergence of new qualities as one moved from atomic, to molecular, to organic, finally, to human social phenomena. He understood that one could not simply apply the laws found in one area of investigation to the phenomena in another area.

44. *Arkhiv K. Marksa i F. Engel'sa,* David Riazanov, ed. (Moscow: Gosudarstvennoe izdatel'stvo, 1925), 2:220–29. The essay (included as chapter 8) is printed in both Russian and German.

45. Trotsky, *The History of the Russian Revolution,* Max Eastman, tr. (Ann Arbor: University of Michigan Press, 1932), 3 vols., 3:276.

46. Trotsky, *Sochineniia,* 21:277–78. Trotsky also persisted in his effort to derive qualitative leaps from the accumulation of slight variations in Darwin's theory.

47. *Ibid.,* p. 333.

48. *Arkhiv K. Marksa i F. Engel'sa,* 2:228–29.

49. *Ibid.,* pp. 226–27.

50. Trotsky, *Sochineniia,* 21:429.

51. See the text, p. 77.

52. See the text, p. 88.

53. See the text, pp. 88–89.

54. See the text, p. 92.

55. See the text, p. 92. I have taken a small liberty with it.

56. See the text, p. 91.

57. See the text, pp. 95–96.

58. See, for example, F. Engels, *Dialectics of Nature* (New York: International Publishers, 1963), pp. 26ff.

Notes: Dialectics 163

59. N. Bukharin, *Historical Materialism* (New York: International Publishers, 1925). Bukharin's system owes a great deal to the inspiration of A. Bogdanov (A. A. Malinovskii). For a good summary of Bogdanov's systemic theory see *Russian Philosophy,* James M. Edie et al., eds., 3 vols. (Knoxville: University of Tennessee Press, 1976), 3:390–404.

60. Bukharin, *Historical Materialism*, p. 74.

61. Another illustration reveals that the Bogdanov-Bukharin translation is still appealing. In a recent review, biologist Stephen J. Gould wrote:

When presented as guidelines for a philosophy of change, not as dogmatic precepts true by fiat, the three classical laws of dialectics—as reflected in the analysis of this book—embody a holistic vision that views change as interaction among components of complete systems, and sees the components themselves not as a priori entities, but as both products of and inputs to the system. Thus, the law of "interpenetrating opposites" is about inextricable interdependence of components; that of "transformation of quantity into quality" about a systems-based view of change that translates incremental inputs into alterations of state; and that of "negation of negation" about the direction given to history because complex systems cannot revert exactly to previous states.

"Between You and Your Genes," *New York Review of Books* (August 16, 1984), 31(13):32.

62. See the text, p. 101.

63. *Russian Philosophy,* James M. Edie et al., eds., 3 vols. (Knoxville: University of Tennessee Press, 1976), 3:438.

64. *Ibid.,* p. 446.

65. *Ibid.,* p. 451.

66. See, for example, G. Wetter, *Dialectical Materialism,* Peter Heath, tr. (London: Routledge and Kegan Paul, 1958), pp. 110–27, 143–49; Loren R. Graham, *Science and Philosophy in the Soviet Union* (New York: Knopf, 1972), chapter 2.

67. Both are reprinted in Trotsky, *In Defense of Marxism,* pp. 48–52, 72–94.

68. *Ibid.,* p. 51.

69. *Ibid.,* p. 74.

70. *Ibid.,* p. 84. Trotsky is clearly being sarcastic, but the position is still problematic. In her article cited above, Paul takes Trotsky (and others as well) to task for his ontological position and uses a portion of the passage just quoted against him. See "Marxism, Darwinism," p. 127.

71. See p. 102.

72. S. Freud, *The Standard Edition of the Complete Works of Sigmund Freud,* James Strachey, tr. and ed., 24 vols. (London: Hogarth Press and the Institute of Psychoanalysis, 1953–), 22:177.

73. Eastman, *Einstein, Trotsky, Hemingway, Freud,* p. 124; Diggins, *Up from Communism,* p. 152.

74. Trotsky, *Trotsky's Diary in Exile,* pp. 166, 167.

75. Trotsky's cryptogenic fevers have been the source of much speculation. He revealed in his autobiography that even as a child he had been prone to fevers, stomach ailments, and headaches (*My Life,* pp. 35, 72–73). He stated frankly that "nervous shocks nearly always affected his digestion." He even had to interrupt his fourth-grade studies because of illness. Yet Trotsky did not speculate about the connection between his "accidents," mysterious fevers, and the political pressures he had faced during the 1920s. He provides readers with material for speculation in *My Life,* pp. 470, 498–500, 508–9. In a letter of September 21, 1933, Trotsky's secretary, Sarah Weber, wrote to Max Eastman

that Trotsky had been examined for malaria recently, but that no evidence for the disease had been found. She added that "as a matter of fact they were never found before" (bMsRuss13.1 T2[11166–67]).

76. See the text, p. 106.

77. Trotsky, *Literature and Revolution* (New York: International Publishers, 1925), pp. 254–55.

78. Trotsky Archives, T3469, pp.8–9.

79. See the text, p. 107.

80. This is my own modified translation of the material that appears in *My Life*, pp. 295–96. It is based upon the published Russian text: Trotsky, *Moia zhizn'* (Berlin, 1930), 2 vols., 2:15–16.

81. Trotsky Archives, T3264 (2 of 6, p. 15).

82. Trotsky, *Moia zhizn'*, 2:56.

83. Trotsky Archives, T3265 (5 of 6, p. 2), manuscript for chapter 29.

84. See the text, p. 102.

Annotations to the English Translations

1. Trotsky no doubt has in mind not only Eastman and Dewey's school of pragmatism, but the English tradition of empiricism. He does not attempt to engage Bertrand Russell and "logical empiricism," which deals with the issue he raises here.

2. The word "concept" is the translation of "poniatie," and the latter is the Russian translation of the German "Begriff." The word "Begriff" is often translated as "notion" in English, but "concept" will be used here.

3. G. F. W. Hegel, *Wissenschaft der Logik,* Georg Lasson, ed., in *Sämtliche Werke* (Leipzig: Felix Meiner, 1923), vol. 3, erster Teil. The quotation is inexact in that a comma has been omitted after "tot."

4. *Ibid.* A comma has been omitted after "Wahrheit."

5. *Ibid.,* p. 44.

6. N. K. Mikhailovskii (1842–1904), a leading Russian literary critic and one of the founders of the Russian school of subjective sociology during the late 1860s, became an object of scorn during the mid-1890s, when Lenin and other Marxists attacked the theoretical founders of Russian populism.

7. Here Trotsky has in mind the well-known Hegelian triad of thesis, antithesis, and synthesis.

8. Trotsky is probably referring to a meeting of the Council of the Russian Social Democratic Workers' Party (RSDRP) that took place in Geneva, Switzerland, and conducted its business in two sessions, May 31 and June 5, 1904 (June 13 and 18 according to the Gregorian calendar). The council sessions were attended by Lenin, Martov, Plekhanov, Aksel'rod, and V. A. Noskov. It is not clear what session Trotsky had in mind, but during the second session the Mensheviks prevailed in the debates over intraparty arrangements. The passage is somewhat obscure because of Trotsky's slipping into the first person. It seems likely that he had intended to refer to Lenin's doubts, for Lenin during this period in 1904 had been unable to control either the council or the Central Committee of the party, although the latter was composed of Bolsheviks.

9. L. Martov (Iu. O. Tsederbaum) had been Lenin's close comrade in arms in

the St. Petersburg Union of Struggle for the Liberation of the Working Class. Both of them were arrested during the crackdown of 1895–96 and then exiled, and both collaborated on *Iskra* from 1900 to 1903, but they clashed during the Second Party Congress in 1903 and became the heads of their respective factions, Martov of the Mensheviks. After returning to Russia in 1917 after the February revolution, Martov opposed the Bolshevik seizure of power and emigrated again in 1920, where he continued his attacks from Berlin. He died there in 1923.

10. Alexander Il'ich Ulianov (1866–1887) was Lenin's older brother. A brilliant zoology student in St. Petersburg University, he became involved in a plot to assassinate Alexander III. The plot was uncovered and Alexander Ulianov was hanged on March 1, 1887. The death of his older brother undoubtedly affected Lenin's choice of a revolutionary career. Trotsky's book on Lenin covering the period 1870 to 1893, *The Young Lenin*, contains an illuminating analysis of the relationship between the two brothers.

11. Trotsky is probably referring to two well-known photographs of Lenin which are reproduced, among other places, in Bertram Wolfe's *Three Who Made a Revolution* (New York: Dell, 1964).

12. S. Ia. Alliluev (1866–1945) was a member of the Bolshevik party whose daughter later married Stalin. He frequently hid Party members on the run from the police in his apartment. Trotsky gives the initial date as July 6 (19), but an authoritative source places Lenin at the apartment of N. G. Poletaev on the night of July 6 (19)–July 7 (20). He moved to Alliluev's apartment on July 7 and stayed there until the night of July 9 (22)–July 10 (23), when he traveled in the company of G. E. Zinoviev and N. A. Emelianov, a worker from Sestroretsk, to Razliv, north of Petrograd and on the Gulf of Finland.

13. Trotsky is referring to a town near Petrograd (St. Petersburg) with a munitions factory and a soviet. It was in the vicinity of Razliv.

14. Beklin is a transliteration from the Russian. The artist referred to is Arnold Böcklin (1827–1901), a Swiss painter. There is a reproduction of the painting described by Trotsky in Rolf Andree, *Arnold Böcklin, die Gemälde* (Basel: Friedrich Reinhardt, 1977), p. 353. The title of the painting, which was done in 1872, is *Self-Portrait with Death Fiddling*. It seems unlikely that Trotsky could have described it in such detail from a snapshot alone.

15. Roman Malinovsky (1876–1918), of Polish birth, after involvement with the Metalworkers Union in St. Petersburg during 1905–10, became a police informer in 1910 (if not earlier). He impressed Lenin in 1912 at the Sixth All-Russian conference of the RSDRP and became a Bolshevik delegate to the Fourth Duma in 1912. He also collaborated on the Party newspaper, *Pravda*. One of Lenin's most trusted helpers, he actually led the Bolshevik delegation in the Duma in 1913–14 until he resigned in May 1914. Despite accurate rumors about Malinovsky, Lenin defended him. During the First World War, Malinovsky again served Lenin, even while a prisoner of war. After the February revolution he was exposed decisively and was executed in November 1918.

16. The diagram to which Trotsky refers was drawn up by one Rozhanov, a police official. It begins in 1762 and ends in 1913, tracing the genealogies of the RSDRP and Socialist-Revolutionary party.

17. This was one of the Bolshevik slogans referring to the Provisional Government formed in March 1917 and calling for its downfall in June 1917 during a massive demonstration in the streets of Petrograd.

18. The reference is to the "police socialism" practiced by S. V. Zubatov (1864–1917), which was a government-sponsored form of unionism designed by the police. While

Annotations to Translations

chief of the Moscow Okhrana (security police) Zubatov founded the Moscow Society for the Mutual Aid of Workers in the Mechanical Industries in 1901. His efforts in behalf of the workers and the success of the organization in southern Russia yielded, in the end, a massive strike movement in 1903. In short, the Zubatov movement backfired and Zubatov was dismissed. The suffix "shchina" appended to his name has strong negative connotations in Russian.

19. "Exes" refers to the expropriations carried out during 1906–8 by the Bolsheviks, sometimes in conjunction with the Maximalist wing of the Socialist-Revolutionary party, despite the disapproval of the Central Committee of the RSDRP. Lenin had no compunctions about the use of violence or deceit to acquire funds—hence the stigmas.

20. V. M. Abrosimov (b. 1878) was an Okhrana agent who collaborated on the Menshevik journals, *Nasha zaria* and *Luch'*.

21. Trotsky here refers to the examination that Lenin took as an external student of the faculty of law at the University of St. Petersburg. He passed his examinations in 1891 with the highest honors, even though he had spent less than two years at a program of study that usually required four and did so without the benefit of instruction. His brief career at law was undistinguished.

22. Vera Ivanovna Zasulich (1849–1919) began her revolutionary career during the Nechaev affair of 1869–70. She created a sensation by wounding the chief of police of St. Petersburg in 1878. After trial and acquittal under the new liberal judiciary, she fled Russia in 1880. In 1883 she became one of the early converts to Marxism and one of the founders of the Group for the Liberation of Labor based in Switzerland. When *Iskra* was founded in 1900, she joined the editorial board. She became an opponent of Lenin after the split in the Party and died unreconciled to the Bolshevik seizure of power.

23. The journals named here were published abroad. *Iskra* was founded in 1900 and between 1900 and 1903 was published in Leipzig, Munich, London, and Geneva. It was the standard-bearer of the RSDRP. After the split at the Second Congress of the RSDRP it became a predominantly Menshevik journal. It ceased publication in 1905, although the Menshevik-Internationalists headed by Martov issued a journal with that title in the autumn of 1917 in Petrograd. During the early history of the RSDRP, *Zaria* was published in Stuttgart in 1901–2 as a sister journal to *Iskra* and concerned itself with theoretical issues. It is not to be confused with the Menshevik émigré journal of the same title published in Berlin in 1922–25. Trotsky has in mind Plekhanov, Aksel'rod, Martov, Zasulich, and himself.

24. Trotsky is referring to 1904 and after, when Lenin attracted new people to his position. A. A. Bogdanov (1873–1928), a man of wide learning whose philosophy had considerable influence in the Party, even though seen by Lenin as heretical, was on the editorial board of the Bolshevik journals *Vpered* and *Proletarii*. Lenin attacked Bogdanov, among others, in *Materialism and Empirio-Criticism* in 1909. After the Revolution he once again antagonized Lenin by being a proponent of a new proletarian cultural movement. M. Ol'minskii (1863–1933) began his long revolutionary career as a populist in the 1880s. He too belonged to the editorial staff of the Bolshevik journals named above and others. He served in several areas and ended his career as the editor of the journal *Proletarskaia revoliutsiia* and as a director of the Institute of V. I. Lenin. A. V. Lunacharskii (1875–1933) had a career in some ways similar to Bogdanov's. After joining Lenin and serving on the Party journals, he too became a heretic and experienced Lenin's wrath in 1909. During the spring and summer of 1917 he and Trotsky belonged to the "Interdistrict" group and, like Trotsky, he joined the Bolsheviks later that year. He was the Soviet Union's

first commissar of education (1917–29). V. V. Vorovskii (1871–1923) began his revolutionary career in 1890 and, like Lenin and Martov, belonged to the Union for the Liberation of the Working Class in St. Petersburg. He actively supported Lenin's position and became his coeditor on Bolshevik journals. He served as a diplomat after 1917 until his assassination in Switzerland. Trotsky's brief dismissal of these men does not so much signify contempt for them as nostalgia for the old *Iskra* before the split.

25. "N. Lenin" was V. I. Ulianov's most frequently used pseudonym. It appears on works dating from February 1902 to March 1923. It was often spelled out "Nikolai Lenin."

26. Nadezhda Konstantinovna Krupskaia (1869–1939) was Lenin's constant companion after their marriage in July 1899. She served as secretary of Lenin's journals throughout his exile abroad and after 1917 became a prominent functionary in the area of education. During Lenin's illness in 1922–24 and after his death, she was treated roughly by Stalin, but in the end submitted to party discipline—which meant to Stalin's policies.

27. Karl Kautsky (1854–1938) was the most respected theoretician in the German social democratic movement during the period of Lenin's apprenticeship and early career. Like others whom Lenin had previously admired, he became an object of bitter scorn during the First World War. August Bebel (1840–1913), a German social democratic leader of working class origin and one of the founders of the Party, was a proponent of revolutionary Marxism during the time when Lenin was also struggling against revisionism. Later, Lenin found him insufficiently radical, as Trotsky's remark suggests.

28. The three names are nicknames. "Lepesha" is N. P. Lepeshinskii (1868–1944). He was in Ekaterinoslav and St. Petersburg in 1905–7; "Rapoposhka" is probably Charles Rappoport, a French social democrat of Russian birth; "Martushka" is Martov.

29. This was a social democratic group (1900–3) made up of D. Riazanov, Iu. M. Steklov, and E. L. Gurevich. Trotsky refers to Lenin's early position on the agrarian question, in which he proposed that the peasants be given the "cutoffs" that had been taken from them after the land settlement connected with the abolition of serfdom in 1861.

30. Wilhelm Liebknecht (1826–1900) belonged to the radical wing of German social democracy and was a comrade in arms of August Bebel. Liebknecht edited the organ of the Party, *Vorwärts,* and was a member of the Second International.

31. F. I. Tiutchev (1803–1873), a lyric poet, believed in Russia's mission to avoid the fate of the West. He belonged to the Slavophile tradition.

32. S. G. Nechaev (1847–1882) had come to stand for unscrupulousness in revolutionary affairs. For a discussion of his appearance in the notebooks see chapter 1.

33. "Kamo" was the revolutionary nickname of S. A. Ter-Petrosyan (1882–1922); he is also discussed in chapter 1.

34. Trotsky is referring to Lenin's older sister, Anna (1864–1935); his younger sister, Mariia (1878–1937); and his younger brother, Dmitrii (1873–1943).

35. The People's Will was the first effective terrorist organization in the history of the Russian revolutionary movement. It organized the assassination of Alexander II on March 1 (13), 1881. By 1883 its executive committee was effectively destroyed, but the tradition continued and fully revived with the Socialist-Revolutionary party during the early years of the twentieth century.

36. Carolus Linnaeus (1707–1778), a Swedish botanist, created modern taxonomy. To Trotsky he represents a static, ahistorical approach to nature.

37. The image of the impermeable or watertight bulkhead is taken from ship-build-

Annotations to Translations 169

ing, an area in which the Anglo-Saxons had traditionally enjoyed superiority. In this case, of course, Trotsky is using heavy irony.

38. The quotation is from Goethe and is used in shorter form in Trotsky, *The History of the Russian Revolution,* Max Eastman, tr. (Ann Arbor: University of Michigan Press, 1932), 3 vols., 1:94.

39. For a possible source of this position, see I. Luppol, "Lenin v bor'be za dialekticheskii materializm," *Molodaia gvardiia* (1924), 2–3:355–56.

40. The article on Fermi entitled "Astonishing Discovery by an Italian Scientist" describes the announcement of Fermi's creation of a new element, uranium 93. Trotsky had long understood the implications of atomic theory and believed that the transmutation of elements by artificial methods signified greater human control over nature and access to the vast stores of energy within the atom. Trotsky also greeted new discoveries of this sort as confirmation of dialectical materialism. (I have not determined the source of the clipping, but the announcement of Fermi's discovery was carried in many newspapers on or shortly after June 5, 1934.)

41. D. I. Mendeleev (1834–1907) discovered the relationships among the elements that led to his formulation of the periodic table of elements.

42. Trotsky refers here to the huge hydroelectric project on the Dnepr in the Ukraine (1927–32).

43. F. I. Dan (1871–1947), a prominent Menshevik and close collaborator with Martov, was a leading proponent of "defensism" during the First World War. He was exiled in 1922 and died an émigré.

44. The reference is to a prominent liberal journal published in Russia (1866–1918).

45. Georges Clemenceau (1841–1929), a leading member of the French Radical party, became premier and minister of war in 1917. Clemenceau's *In the Evening of My Thought* (Boston: Houghton Mifflin, 1929) sets forth his views on evolution at considerable length.

46. Trotsky probably had in mind the well-known paradox (aporia) attributed to the Greek school of thought at Megara (late 5th–early 3rd century B.C.).

47. Hegel, *Wissenschaft der Logik,* erster Teil, pp. 26–27.

48. *Ibid.,* p. 28.

49. Trotsky, of course, had in mind Max Eastman (1883–1969) and Eastman's attack upon dialectics, discussed in chapter 1.

50. This theory was the product of the joint efforts of Immanuel Kant (1724–1804) and Pierre Simon Laplace (1749–1827). They believed the solar system was a product of nebular evolution—of the condensation of gases.

51. Sir Charles Lyell (1797–1875), a British geologist, made a major contribution to the formulation of modern evolutionism through his studies of rock strata and his work in palaeontology.

52. G. V. Plekhanov (1856–1918) is considered to be the father of Russian Marxism. He began his revolutionary career as a populist during the 1870s and emigrated after the split in the populist movement over the strategy of terrorism. In emigration he converted to Marxism and became the leading figure in the Group for the Liberation of Labor in Geneva, Switzerland. He remained a leading theoretician after the formation of the RSDRP and the splits. Like the Mensheviks, to whom he was closer than to the Bolsheviks, he opposed Lenin's seizure of power.

53. Hegel, *Wissenschaft der Logik,* erster Teil, p. 60.

54. The announcement entitled "The Third Centenary of *Discourse on Method*"

refers to the decision of the eighth International Congress of Philosophy to dedicate the ninth congress to Descartes. It would be convened in Paris in 1937. The announcement appeared in *Le Temps* (Paris), February 19, 1935, p. 3. Cartesianism, of course, belonged to a philosophical tradition uncongenial to dialecticians.

55. The English translation of Wittels' book is *Sigmund Freud: His Personality, His Teaching, and His School,* Eden and Cedar Paul, tr. (New York: Dodd, Mead, 1924). It is possible that Trotsky's remarks about Freud's theory of primitive languages are based upon chapter 16, "Bipolarity." There Wittels mentions Freud's interest in the philologist Karl Abel's theory of the antithetical sense of primal words and discusses the theory briefly.

56. S. L. Kliachko (1850–1914) began his long revolutionary career in the 1870s as a member of the Chaikovskii circle in Moscow. He spent most of his life as an émigré and died in Vienna.

57. A. I. Herzen (1812–1870), one of Russia's earliest and most distinguished socialist thinkers, during his longer career as an émigré (1847–70) became an idol of the younger generation of radicals. His influence reached its height during the late 1850s and early 1860s when the journal *Kolokol,* published in London, both reflected and inspired the mood of those opposed to the Tsarist regime.

58. Hugo De Vries (1848–1935), a Dutch botanist, whose theory of mutation evidently troubled Trotsky much as it troubled other dialecticians. Apparently Trotsky objected to the idea that variations could not acquire the status of species. Trotsky's approach, which presupposed an accumulation of small changes, differed from the theory of mutations, and he seemingly rejected this path to speciation. For the reaction of other Marxists to De Vries, see Diane B. Paul, "Marxism, Darwinism, and the Theory of Two Sciences," *Marxist Perspectives* (Spring 1979), 2:125–26.

59. The quotation from Alfred Russel Wallace is in Russian, and Trotsky did not cite the work from which he took it. I present Wallace's original version below. Trotsky's stylistic changes and use of ellipses account for the differences in the two English texts.

Far abler men than myself may confess, that they have not that untiring patience in accumulating, and that wonderful skill in using, large masses of facts of the most varied kind,—that wide and accurate physiological knowledge,—that astuteness in devising and skill in carrying out experiments,—and that admirable style of composition, at once clear, persuasive and judicial,—qualities, which in their harmonious combination mark out Mr. Darwin as the man, perhaps of all men now living, best fitted for the great work he has undertaken and accomplished.

A. R. Wallace, *On Natural Selection* (London: Macmillan, 1870), pp. iv–v.

Index

"ABC of Materialist Dialectics, The" (Trotsky), 63
Abrosimov, V. M., 80
Aksel'rod, P. B., 7, 47, 108
Alliluev, S. Ia., 12
Alma Ata, 13
Anarchism, 79
Animism, 42, 46; in Trotsky, 54, 72; and dialectics, 65; *see also* Anthropomorphism
Anthropomorphism, 42, 46, 54; in Darwin, 51; *see also* Animism
Antinomies, 90, 93, 109
Apparatus, the (CPSU), 12, 27, 28, 86
Aristotelian syllogism, 99
Aristotle, 40, 99
"Arts and Letters under Stalin" (Eastman), 45

Bakunin, M. A., 30
Bebel, August, 82
Beklin, *see* Böcklin, Arnold
Bismarck, Otto von, 80
Blanqui, L. A., 81
Böcklin, Arnold, 80
Bogdanov, A. A., 81
Bolsheviks, 8, 24, 33, 55; in 1917, 10; and Trotsky, 11
Bolshevism, 31; origin of, 7; and terrorism, 30
Boni, Charles, 177*n*10
Bor'ba (Struggle), 84
Brest-Litovsk, Treaty of (1918), 11, 23

Bronstein, Lev Davidovich, *see* Trotsky, L. D.
Bukharin, N. I., 32, 108; as dialectician, 41, 59, 60, 62, 72; and evolutionism, 48; and Trotsky, 59–60
Bulletin of the Opposition, 14
Burnham, James, 38, 45, 63

Catastrophism, 161–62*n*35
"Catechism of a Revolutionary" (Bakunin and Nechaev), 30–31
Catherine II, 80
Central Committee: Bolshevik, 10–11; of the CPSU, 12; and Lenin, 23; of the RSDRP, 167*n*19
Centralism: bureaucratic, 33; Leninist, 33
Cicero, 111
Civil War, Russian, 11, 17, 23, 31
Clemenceau, Georges, 97
Cognition, 75, 77–78, 88, 97–99; catastrophic principle in, 101; dialectic of, 101–2; *see also* Consciousness
Communist Party of the Soviet Union (CPSU), 12
Consciousness, 54, 64, 67, 77–78; and Marxism, 70; origin of, 97; dialectic of, 101; and nature, 101–2; and brain physiology, 104, 106–7; autonomy of, 106–7
Constituent Assembly, the, 23
Copenhagen, 67
Cosmology, 112
Council (RSDRP), *see* Russian Social Democratic Workers' Party
"Culture and Socialism" (Trotsky), 52

Index

Dan, F. I., 95
Darwin, Charles, 42, 46, 51, 68, 99, 104, 108, 111; and dialectics, 51; and English thought, 89; and A. R. Wallace, 114
Darwinism, 89, 96, 109, 113–14; and dialectics, 47–48, 50–51, 63, 87; bourgeois elements in, 51; social, 51; and genius, 84; and National Socialism, 94
Descartes, René, 2, 40, 103–4
Determinism, 113–14
Deutscher, Isaac, 20, 37, 40, 157n10
De Vries, Hugo, 114
Dewey, John, 41–42
Dialectical materialism, 37, 42, 87, 96–97, 109; and psychology, 106
Dialectics, 18, 75; and animism, 42–43, 65; and Darwinism, 47, 51, 87; laws of, 48, 50, 53, 62–65, 87–88, 90, 92; unconscious, 52, 55, 63–64, 66, 91–92; styles of, 55–56, 58; architectonics of, 57; and epigenetic principle, 57, 60–61; and conflict, 57; and systemic principle, 57, 60–61; and catastrophic principle, 58, 60–61, 71, 90–91; and genetic principle, 58, 71; and metaphors, 58, triad in, 59, 99; and psychoanalysis, 68; and the unconscious, 71; and formal logic, 86–87, 97–99, 111; and evolutionism, 88, 96, 98; and English thought, 89; and cognition, 101; reversals in, 109–10
Diggins, John P., 160n18
Discourse on Method (Descartes), 2, 103–4

Eastman, Elena, 44
Eastman, Max, 14, 18–19, 41, 61, 63, 72, 98, 112, 161n27; on Lenin, 17, 43; and Trotsky, 17, 44–45, 47; on dialectics, 42–43; on Marxism, 44; and Freud, 64–65
Empiricism, 159n4, 165n1
Engels, Friedrich, 50, 52, 89, 108; as dialectician, 57; his theory of the state, 94–95; and evolutionism, 98
Essays on the Materialistic Conception of History (Labriola), 39
Eugenics, 66
Evolution, 116
Evolutionism, 18, 46, 96–98, 161–62n35; Trotsky's theory of, 109; *see also* Darwin; Darwinism; Gould, Stephen J.

Fascism, Italian, 94
Fermi, Enrico, 2, 92
Fetter, F., 108
Feuilleton de Temps, 109
Fourth International, 14
French Revolution, 99
Freud, Sigmund, 42, 49, 67–68, 106; his theory of the unconscious, 54; on Hegel, 64–65; on Marx, 64–65; his theory of language, 89–90; and Eastman, 64–65
Freud, l'homme, la doctrine, l'école (Wittels), 106

Galileo, 112
"General Character of the Dialectic as Science, The" (Engels), 50
Genetics, 26
Genius, 84
Gould, Stephen J., 163n61
Gurevich, E. L., 168n29

Hegel, G. W. F., 1, 39–41, 99, 111–12; and animism, 42, 54; as dialectician, 53, 57, 75, 77, 88–89; triad in, 60, 78; idealism of, 64, 78, 98; on Kant, 77; and Kant-Laplace theory, 89
Helphand, Alexander (Parvus), 8–9
Herzen, A. I., 111
Historical materialism, 26; *see also* Dialectical materialism
Historical Materialism (Bukharin), 59–60
History of the Russian Revolution (Trotsky), 13, 18–19, 25, 44, 50
Hitler, Adolf, 22
Hook, Sidney, 63

Idealism, 87; in psychoanalysis, 106; *see also* Hegel, idealism of
Imperialism: Lenin's theory of, 9
In Defense of Marxism (Trotsky), 38
Intelligentsia: the Russian, 86, 94; the workers', 94
Iskra (Spark), 7–8, 81, 86

Index

Joint Opposition, the, 13

Kamenev, L. B., 12
Kamo, *see* Ter-Petrosyan, S. A.
Kant, Immanuel, 77, 99
Kantianism, 87
Kant-Laplace theory, the, 88-89, 99, 104
Kareev, N., 108
Kautsky, Karl, 47, 50, 60, 82, 109
Kliachko, S. L., 111
Knei-Paz, Baruch, 40, 157n10
Krasnaia letopis' (Red Chronicle), 80
Kronstadt mutiny (1921), 11-12
Krupskaia, N. K., 81

Labriola, Antonio, 39
Lenin, V. I. (Ulianov): Trotsky's biography of, 4; Jacobinism of, 7; and Trotsky, before 1917, 9; and Trotsky during World War I, 10; and Bolshevik Central Committee, 11, 24, 83; and NEP, 12; and Stalin (1922-23), 12; death of (1924), 13; "Testament" of, 13; and Mensheviks (1904), 18; in the October Revolution, 19, 21-22, 35, 80; and the CPSU, 20; and the apparatus of the CPSU, 27-28, 86; and Nechaev, 29, 85; and Ter-Petrosyan (Kamo), 29, 85; and revolutionary terror, 30; and the split in the RSDRP, 31; centralism of, 32-33; as philosopher, 38-39, 42; as dialectician, 41, 43, 55-56, 58, 60-62, 72, 87, 94-96, 102; and Martov, 54-55, 79, 83, 94-96; on Hegel, 61-62; in 1907-10, 80; handwriting of, 81; as law student, 81; pseudonym of, 81; and Bebel, 82; and Kautsky, 82; in 1915, 82; in 1921, 82; psychology of, 83-84, 86; mistakes of, 84; and Stalin, 86; as politician, 96; *see also* Leninism
"Lenin and the Epigones," (Trotsky), 17
Leninism, 27, 31
Leninskii sbornik, 39
Lepeshinskii, N. P. (Lepesha), 83
"Lessons of October" (Trotsky), 23
Liebknecht, Wilhelm, 85
Linnaeus, Carolus, 87, 114
Literature and Revolution (Trotsky), 37, 49, 66

Logic, 38, 75, 86-87, 99; syllogistic, 91, 111
Ludwig, Emil, 25, 26
Lunacharskii, A. V., 81
Luppol, I., 108
Lyell, Charles, 99, 104

Makers of Modern Europe (Sforza), 17
Malamuth, Charles, 5
Malinovsky, Roman, 80
Malthusianism, 51
Marcuse, Herbert, 72
Martov, Iu. O. (Tsederbaum), 7, 10, 19, 34, 77; editor of *Iskra,* 8; and Lenin, 54; as dialectician, 55, 58, 94-96; psychology of, 83; as politician, 96
Marx, Karl, 42, 44, 68, 99, 104; on Darwin, 51; as dialectician, 52; on Hegel, 112; *see also* Marxism
Marx and Lenin: The Science of Revolution (Eastman), 16, 41, 65
Marxism, 14, 70, 89, 96; Eastman's critique of, 17; Russian, 23, 31, 67, 103-4; and Darwinism, 49, 51; and National Socialism, 94; Legal, 103-4
Materialism, 77, 96; *see also* Dialectical materialism; Historical materialism
Materialism and Empirico-Criticism (Lenin), 39, 61
Maurois, André (Herzog), 25
Mendeleev, D. I., 49, 52, 68, 92, 111, 113
"Mendeleev and Marxism" (Trotsky), 49-50
Mendelian genetics, 26
Mensheviks, 8, 18, 55, 94, 110
Menshevism, origin of, 8
Messianism, 84
Mikhailovskii, N. K., 78, 108
Military Revolutionary Committee, 10
Mill, John Stuart, 91, 97
Moscow Insurrection (1905), 24, 82-83
My Life (Trotsky), 13-14, 25, 34, 37, 69, 70-72

Narodnaia Volia (The People's Will), 86
National Socialism, 93; and dialectics, 94; and Darwinism, 116; *see also* Nazism
Natural selection, 113
Nature, dialectic in, 101

Index

Naturdialektik (Engels), 50, 52
Nashe slovo (Our Word), 10
Nazism, 22
Nechaev, S. G., 29–31; and Lenin, 33, 84
Nechaevshchina, 30
Nevskii, B., 108
New Economic Policy (NEP), 11
New York Times, 109
Nicholas II, Tsar, 8
Novack, George, 157*n*10, 161*n*28
Novyi mir (New World), 10

October Revolution, the (1917), 10, 19–21; *see also* Russian Revolution, the
Ol'minskii, M. S., 81
O'Neill, William, 160*n*18
On Lenin (Trotsky), 23
"Open Letter to Comrade Burnham" (Trotsky), 58
Our Political Tasks (Trotsky), 31

Paleontology, 114
Parvus, A., *see* Helphand, A.
Paul, Diane B., 162*n*35, 170*n*58
Pavlov, I. P., 49
Permanent revolution: theory of, 9
Petrograd, 69
Petrograd Soviet, 10
Phenomenology of Mind (Hegel), 54
Philosophical Notebooks (Lenin), 4, 39, 60–62
Philosophy of science, 50
Plekhanov, G. V., 7, 19, 47, 84–85, 102, 108
Politburo (CPSU), 12–13
Populism, Russian, 14
Positivism, 91
Potresov, A. N., 7
Pravda (1908–12), 9
Prinkipo (Turkey), 13–14, 22, 44, 67
Proletarskaia revoliutsiia (Proletarian Revolution), 82
Provisional Government, Russian, in 1917, 23, 166*n*17
Psychoanalysis, 26, 42, 68, 72; Trotsky on, 66; and dialectical materialism, 106; and idealism, 106
Psychology, 49; and dialectical materialism, 106

Rappoport, Charles (Rapoposhka), 83
Rationalism, 99
Red Army, the, 11, 69
Revolution Betrayed, The (Trotsky), 20
Revolutionary Military Council, 13
Riazanov, David, 50, 168*n*29
Russell, Bertrand, 165*n*1
"Russian Darwin, A" (Trotsky), 46
Russian Revolution, the: of 1905, 9; of 1917, 15, 21, 26, 67, 84; *see also* October Revolution, the
Russian Social Democratic Workers' Party (RSDRP), 7, 31; Council of, 79; *see also* Central Committee (RSDRP)

St. Petersburg Soviet (1905), Trotsky and, 8
Science of Logic, The (Hegel), see *Wissenschaft der Logik*
Scientific revolutions, 53
Second International, the, 10, 82
Sedova, Natalia, 9–10, 22
Sforza, Carlo, 17–18, 21
Shachtman, Max, 38, 45
Slavophilism, 85
Social and Political Thought of Leon Trotsky, The (Knei-Paz), 40
Socialist Revolutionary party, the, 167*n*19
Sokolovskaia, Alexandra, 7
Solov'ev, T. P., 46
South Russian Workers' Union, 7
Speciation, 114
Stalin, J. V. (Dzhugashvili), 18, 110; and Trotsky (1918–21), 11; and Central Committee (CPSU), 12; as Commissar of Nationalities, 12; and the apparatus (CPSU), 13, 27–28, 86; Trotsky's biography of, 20; and terror, 30; ruthlessness of, 31; on Trotsky, 32
Stalinism, 27, 31
Stalin's Russia and the Crisis in Socialism (Eastman), 45
Steklov, Iu. M., 168*n*29
Stolypin, P. A., 8
Souvarine, Boris, 32
Syllogism, 111; *see also* Logic

Tbilisi (Tiflis), 29

Index

Teleology, 113–14
Ter-Petrosyan, S. A. (Kamo), 29, 85; and Lenin, 33
Terror, 30–31
"Testament": Lenin's, 13; Trotsky's, 34, 47, 65
Timiriazev, K., 108
Tiutchev, F. I., 85
Tolstoy, Leo, 113
Totem and Taboo (Freud), 42
Trotsky, L. D. (Bronstein): his biography of Lenin, 4–5, 17–18, 21–23, 26–27, 29; as philosopher, 4, 38–39; childhood of, 6; education of, 6; Populism of, 6, 14; Marxism of, 6–7, 14; first arrest of (1898), 7; first marriage of, 7; first Siberian exile of (1901–2), 7; and South Russian Workers' Union, 7; and *Iskra*, 7–8; and Bolshevism, 7–8, 10–11, 24, 32, 34; and Menshevism, 7–8; and Helphand, 8; second arrest of (1905), 8; second Siberian exile of (1907), 8; editor of *Pravda* (1908–12), 9; and Lenin before 1917, 9; and psychoanalytic movement, 9; second marriage of, 9; as Commissar of Foreign Affairs, 10–11; and Lenin during World War I, 10; and Lenin in 1917, 10; and Martov, 10, 34; and the October Revolution, 10, 19, 22, 25, 35; and Brest-Litovsk, 11; and NEP, 11–12; and the Russian Civil War, 11; and the Red Army, 11; and Stalin, 11–12; expelled from CPSU (1927), 13; exiled to Alma Ata (1928), 13; exiled to Turkey (1929), 13, 22–23; illness of (1923–24), 13; and Lenin's "Testament," 13; his loss of power, 13; his exile in France, 14; his exile in Norway, 14; his exile in Mexico, 14; and Eastman, 17, 41–42, 44–45; his identification with Lenin, 18, 34–35, 56, 72–73; his notes on Lenin, 18; and CPSU, 23–24; as biographer, 25–26; as historian, 25, 35; and revolutionary terror, 30; on centralism, 32–33; and Leninism, 34; on dialectical materialism, 37–38; and the natural sciences, 38, 108; as dialectician, 41, 45, 49–51, 53, 59–60, 62–63; on psychology, 49, 67; on Darwinism, 50–51; his theory of consciousness, 54; and Bukharin, 59–60; his evolutionism, 109
Trotsky's Diary in Exile, 1935, 3
Tsarism, 86

Ulianov, Alexander, 79
Ulianov, D. I., 86
Ulianov family, 26, 86
Ulianova, A. I., 86
Ulianova, M. I., 86
Unconscious, the, 54, 63–69, 107; and dialectics, 68; in history, 70–71; and revolution, 71; and Marxism, 72

Van Heijenoort, Jean, 3, 37–38, 159n1
Vestnik Evropy (Herald of Europe), 97
La Vie de Lenine: Jeunesse, 23; see also *Young Lenin, The*
Vorovskii, V. V., 80

Wallace, Alfred Russel, 114, 116, 170n59
War Communism, 12
Weber, Sarah, 164n75
Wissenschaft der Logik (Hegel), 1, 39, 61, 75
Wittels, Fritz, 40–41, 66, 106

Young Lenin, The, 30

Zaria (Dawn), 81
Zasulich, V. I., 7, 29, 81
Zimmerwald Conference, the, 10
Zinoviev, G. E., 12, 79
Zubatov, S. V., 80

Printed in Great Britain
by Amazon